Wallsend Shops Past & Present

A trip down shopping's memory lane

By Steve Boundey
On behalf of the Wallsend Local History Society

High Street West in the 1960s with Hadrian's, Ruddick's, Workwear Suppliers, Ainsworth's and Carole's. (This photograph is one of many supplied by Mrs Eileen Williams.)

Previous page: Maypole Dairy Co Ltd, High Street, Wallsend. Most of their butters were nearly all sold loose and was formed into the recognised block from a larger block that came to the shop in a wooden box or barrel. A $^1/_4$ lb or $^1/_2$ lb cut was weighed and patted into shape and wrapped as required. Very few products were pre-packed as they are today.

Front cover: Top – The butchers department of one of the branches of Greenwell's who had several shops in Wallsend and Willington Quay as well as Byker and Walker. *Bottom* – Steve Phillips in his butchers shop on Tynemouth Road, Howdon in 2011.

Copyright Steve Boundey and the Wallsend Local History Society 2011

First published in 2011 by

Summerhill Books
PO Box 1210, Newcastle-upon-Tyne NE99 4AH

www.summerhillbooks.co.uk

email: summerhillbooks@yahoo.co.uk

ISBN: 978-1-906721-46-6

Contents

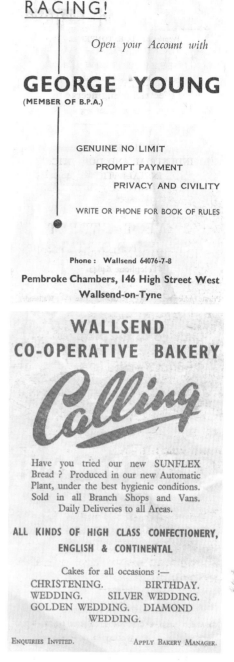

Introduction

The following photographs, adverts and stories are all about the old shops and businesses that have come and gone around Wallsend, Howdon, Rosehill and Willington Quay. There are many photographs or adverts for these shops but there are also a multitude of shops that plied their trade which I have not been able to obtain a picture. It is hoped that just a mention of some of their names will bring the memories flooding back.

Born in 1960, I cannot remember some of the shops, such as those that were demolished to make way for the Wallsend Forum. Members of the Wallsend Local History Society have been asked to cast their minds back and try to remember the old shops and write a short paragraph about them. I, personally, have a few memories, namely of **Ruddick's** the fruit shop on High Street East, where my mother Elsie Boundey used to work and of the barber shop, whose name I cannot remember, located a few doors along from **Ruddick's**. My mother also worked for **Presto's** which stood at the front of Wallsend Forum, opposite the west side of the Anson public house, and also in **Sanderson's** sweet shop on Tynemouth Road, Howdon. I can also remember **Mountford's** television shop and **Brodie's** the grocer's shop which were located on Tynemouth Road. How many people can remember such shops as the **V.G.** on Cleveland Gardens, **Taylor's** sweet shop on Howdon Lane and **Morton's** fish and

chip shop on Tynemouth Road to name but a few. It is hoped that the following pages bring back fond memories to all who have lived and shopped in the Wallsend area.

Our journey starts at the top of High Street West approaching from Newcastle, then on through High Street East, then to the surrounding areas of Wallsend, Willington Quay, through Rosehill and on to Howdon. In Roman times 'High Way' or 'High Street' meant 'main route' or 'main road' and as this was the only road suitable for taking large transport such as horses and carts it was found that it was the most obvious place to start building shops and houses. As Wallsend developed and smaller housing estates were built the shops and businesses started to spread out. The first section contains the shops known to be on both side of High Street West between just west of The Avenue and Station Road.

An attempt has been made to place the shops in the correct order that they would have been in but many adverts or articles where the information has been gathered do not give the door numbers. Of the shops with door numbers there are not that many who have retained the number on the exterior of the shop. Many shop addresses now go by just the name and some have covered up the old names and numbers with big signs so an apology is made here if the shops are not in the correct order.

I hope you enjoy your journey down memory lane.

Steve Boundey, 2011
Wallsend Local History Society

Wallsend Local History Society

Many thanks go to my friends and colleagues of the Wallsend Local History Society for their help with this project. The Society meets in the Memorial Hall, 39 Station Road, Wallsend, on the 2nd Monday of each month at 7 pm to 9 pm.

As well as our well attended monthly meetings we support a wide variety of local interests such as the Wallsend Festival where our stall arouses great interest. Our members also enjoy frequent bus outings.

To find out more about the Society, come along; you'll receive a warm welcome in a friendly atmosphere.

Full membership is £5 per year. This fee covers everything except outings. Visitors, who are most welcome, are charged £1 for the evening. This includes tea and biscuits. There are facilities for disabled persons.

Please visit our newly created website at **www.wallsendhistory.btck.co.uk** and leave your comments in our message book.

This photograph was taken at the Wallsend Local History Society stall in the Forum on Wallsend Festival Day in 2006. The Festival usually takes place on the first Saturday in July and the History Society always provide many interesting old and new photographs and we are proud to say that our stall always seems to be the most popular stall attracting many visitors.

Pictured from left to right are: Ken Hutchinson, Joyce Smith, Don Price, Fiona Jackson, David Corrigil and Edmund Hall.

In memory of Don Price 1939 – 2010
former Secretary of the Wallsend Local History Society
"Time spent relaxing is time wasted."

High Street West

Denney's Motors

When approaching Wallsend from the west, **Denney's Garage** was situated at the junction just west of High Street West and West Street, just before the Duke of York on the northern side of High Street West. **Denney's** used to hire out vehicles of all sizes for all occasions and also used to repair vehicles on their premises and sell petrol. The garage has long gone and on its site now stands **Forster's Garage**. Former employees of **Denney's**, around the years 1954-1962, include my father, Bill Boundey, Neville Worth (Nev), Billy Mees, Norman Yearm (Tucker), Alan Laws, Bill Hails, Cyril Herd, Harry Lochran, Tommy Hodgson who was married to Anne Denney and not forgetting William (Billy) the manager and Lilly Denney. (Hopefully the names have been spelt right – if not an apology is made now). The advert on the right is taken from the 1925 issue of the Guide to Wallsend. (Notice the different spellings of the name **Denney** or **Denny** as it is in the above advert.)

TELEPHONE: 318, WALLSEND.

Denny's Motors, Wallsend.

(PROPRIETORS, J. DENNY & SON).

WEST END GARAGE, HIGH STREET.

NEXT TO ST. AIDAN'S CHURCH.

Touring Cars. Taxis and Lorries for Hire. Repairs of every description by Expert Mechanics. We have most up-to-date MOTOR COACHES for Hire.

Parties, large and small, catered for

Distance no object.

Any make of Car or Motor Cycle supplied.

Bill Denney was the manager and lived on Grassmere Road, in the first house just around the corner from the garage. Also working here was Anne Redgrave, who worked in the office, Marina Webster who was in a Ritz beauty pageant and Jimmy Smith. Also at Denney's Garage were Tommy Henderson and Sidney Holgate. They left **Denney's** and hired a garage at Portugal Place, which was once an abattoir and still had all of the hooks on the wall. This garage was also the start of **2H Taxis** (the 2 H's coming from the initials of Tommy and Sidney's surnames). It was accessed via a tunnel next to the Queens Head public house. The garage is still there to this day but it is now **D.J.M. Coachworks**.

DENNEY'S MOTORS, WALLSEND
FOR
WEDDINGS, CAR VALETING & HIGH PRESSURE WASHING
TELEPHONE 63718

Above: Photo supplied by North Shields Library.

Right: Advert taken from Wallsend Jubilee booklet, 1901-1951. The vehicle in this advert is a Vauxhall Wyvern. The Wyvern is used in the TV series 'Heartbeat' as the taxi cab that David drives.

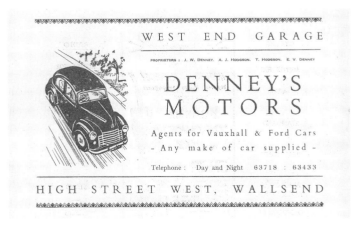

WEST END GARAGE

PROPRIETORS : J. W. DENNEY, A. J. HODGSON, T. HODGSON, E. V. DENNEY

DENNEY'S MOTORS

Agents for Vauxhall & Ford Cars
- Any make of car supplied -

Telephone : Day and Night 63718 : 63433

HIGH STREET WEST, WALLSEND

Boy's Scouts

At the corner of West Street and High Street West used to stand the Boys' Scout hut. This was on a small bit of land before the Duke of York.

J. Moore

Next to the Boys' Scout hut was **J. Moore's Building and Contracting Firm**, which was situated at number 183 on the north side of High Street West. They boasted they would take on jobs of all sizes and many large contracts were undertaken successfully. It was located before the Duke of York public house, which still stands at number 179 High Street West.

A row of houses named York Drive occupy the site between the Duke of York and what is now the **Co-operative Funeral Services**.

Next came the Duke of York public house and just after this was said to have been a pie shop (name not known).

George Romaine

The first shop on Wallsend High Street West, on the south side when entering from the west, was the singer **George Romaine's** shop. It was located approximately on the corner of where Portugal Place joined High Street West, across from Wallsend's first police station and opposite the Duke of York public house.

Do you remember the 'One O'clock Show' hosted by Terry O'Neill with George Romaine, the singer, and the comedian 'Wacky Jacky'? The 'One O'clock Show' was the first TV programme produced in the North East to entertain local people which is why so many can remember it. Kids could watch if they were at home for their lunch. Tyne Tees Television started broadcasting on Thursday, 15th January 1959. The very first programme was at 5 pm and was a fifteen minute opening ceremony conducted by the Duke of Northumberland. From then on Tyne Tees went from strength to strength even collecting a healthy daytime audience with their 'One O'clock Show'.

There is now a ladies hairdresser's shop, **Maze Hairdressing Salon**, on the site of George Romaine's shop.

J. MOORE

Builder & Contractor

183 High St., W.
WALLSEND

Telephone - - Wallsend 323

Residence : 47 ARMSTRONG ROAD
WILLINGTON QUAY

John J. Simpson

John J. Simpson was situated at number 170 on the south side of High Street West. This builder and joiner would have stood practically alongside the pub now named Last Orders around where **Crystal & Son Ltd (Printers)** now stands.

Simpson's would probably have been close competition for **Moore's** a few doors up on the other side of the road if they were in operation at the same time.

R. Peacock

As this shop was numbered 165/7/9 on High Street West, **R. Peacock's** decorators business must have been directly opposite the Last Orders public house, which was probably known as the Anchor Hotel then.

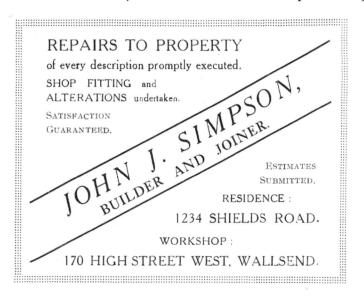

REPAIRS TO PROPERTY
of every description promptly executed.
SHOP FITTING and
ALTERATIONS undertaken.
SATISFACTION
GUARANTEED.

JOHN J. SIMPSON,
BUILDER AND JOINER.

ESTIMATES
SUBMITTED.

RESIDENCE :
1234 SHIELDS ROAD.

WORKSHOP :
170 HIGH STREET WEST, WALLSEND.

Patterson's Second-hand Shop

Thomas W. Patterson's was located on the south side of High Street West, what is now the **Modern Tandoori Restaurant**. It was bought off **Patterson's** by my aunt, Sandra (Lammie) and uncle, John Barron who turned it into the **Costa Brava** Spanish Restaurant which ran from 1992 until 1994. **Patterson's**, a family run second-hand shop specialising in furniture and good second-hand carpets, was first opened in 1918 by Mrs Betty Richardson. Her son, Thomas Patterson (Tot) took over the shop from her and run it until it closed on 16th February 1991. Thomas first worked in the shop in 1934 as soon as he left school, when his father, a French-polisher, died. In the early 1990s it stood next to **Emersons Pet and Garden Centre**, now **Crystal & Son Printers**.

Wilkinson's

Around the early 1850s the shop premises to the west of the then Hare and Hounds public house (the Anchor Hotel in the photo below, now known as Last Orders) was

thought to have been run by **John Wilkinson** from Felling. He ran this grocers shop until around the late 1880s when it was taken over by two Isabellas and a Richard Wilkinson who lasted until the late 1920s. From the beginning of the 1900s the shop, just to the east of the public house, was thought to have been Mary Jane Wilkinson's barber shop and tobacconists. Mary Jane was succeeded by Jack Wilkinson who remained there until the mid 1920s. His son Stan used to work in this barbers shop before he became more popularly known as an insurance agent in the Howdon area. Photo supplied by Malcolm Dunn.

E. Findlay

Although the main Works and Registered Office was located at 56 Clyde Street (*below*), Wallsend, which was roughly where the Forum stands now, decorators **E. Findlay** did

have a shop at 147 High Street West, which is now the site of York Drive on the north side of High Street West. Another competitor to **R. Peacock's** down the road.

J. & W.O. Brown

Although **J. & W.O. Brown's** had a shop on the north side of High Street West at number 143, again where York Drive is now, they also had a property at number 1 Birkett Street, which used to run north to south from Thames Street to High Street West, just east of the Duke of York public house. They also had a property in South Shields at number 23 Victoria Road.

C.A. Lawrence

C.A. Lawrence was a quality baker and confectioner of Wallsend. Located at 135 High Street West; this is now where **Premier** is situated.

McPherson & Kane

At 133 High Street West, **McPherson & Kane's** ladies' and children's outfitters specialised in dresses which may have been made from a high class materials such as silks and wool which they were noted for.

A.W. McCullagh

Located at number 132 High Street West was the saddler, **A.W. McCullagh**. It would probably have stood on the south side of High Street West where **Laavanya's** newsagents shop is on the corner of Border Road, opposite **McPherson and Kane's** outfitters. Not much is known about this saddlers shop but it was not the only leather shop in Wallsend. Due to the fact that most people did not have a great deal of money, these kind of shops would have had a good trade as people could not afford to buy new as much and would have kept taking their belongings to be repaired.

G. Marchi

Not quite a sweet shop but an ice cream parlour. **Marchi's** ice cream was snow white and delicious. You could also sit down for ice cream, coffee, or hot orange on the bench seats each side of about three long marble topped tables. Italo Marchi who owned the ice cream parlour was a driving force behind the project of the opening of a new Catholic club in Wallsend, which opened on 12th December 1966 and is still open in 2011 – the Lindisfarne club on West Street. This is again on the site of York Drive Houses at 125 High Street West.

Backley's (R.L. Blackburn) Ltd

A bakers shop at 120 High Street West, which is covered in more detail on page 23.

Bishop's

Bishop's was a confectioner's shop on the south of High Street West, just west of **Siddle's** newspaper shop. It advertised Cadbury's chocolate in the windows. Also on this photo below can be seen **Greenwell's** store which is now the **Co-operative Funeral Service.**

Siddle

Siddle's newsagents was on the western corner of High Street West, at number 68, and Border Road. It was **Alexander Brooks** around 1925 and is now **Laavanya's** and was still a newsagent shop until 2011 when Laavanya's shop closed.

Next we move to the large array of shops which were located between Border Road and Station Road.

Hardy's Furniture Shop

This shop was located in the same premises now occupied by **Co-operative Funeral Services**. Built in 1926 it is now a grand building at the east end of York Drive. The date is on the drainpipe above the shop windows. The building was thought to have once been **J.R. Greenwell's Ltd**, Provisions Merchants (*below*). Next to **Hardy's**, which later became a shop called **Axe** (it is not known what it sold or when it changed) stood the Robin Hood public house which at one time became Chadwicks and is now the Ship and next to that used to be **Tomms** cycle shop, which took over **Alsop's** cycle shop which is now **Noor Spice**. **Alsop's** was still trading in the 1980s.

Located west of the Black Bull at one time around the late 1920s were the following shops: 99-97, **Sample's**; 95, **G.W. Harrison's**; 93, **Pittuck's**; 91, **M.K. Holmes**; 89, **T.T. Holmes** and at 85 was the Black Bull. **George William Harrison** was trading further down the street as a watchmaker in

1906. He briefly held a few of the shops in this group trading as a musical instrument dealer, cycle dealer and watchmaker and can be traced as late as 1933 at 95 High Street West as a watchmaker and jeweller. **William Sample** took over the cycle business around 1916 and by 1932 this cycle shop had been taken over by **Tomms Cycles** and **Alsop & Sons**. Part of the sign can still be seen today under the Pizza sign of the shop now in its place.

M. Cobden

M. Cobden's Opticians was part of the **Mecca Bingo Hall** building, just on the opposite side of the archway from the Black Bull public house. **Cobden** was said to have retired from the business when this shop closed.

Miss Agnes Pittuck

At number 93 High Street West stood **Miss Pittuck's Opticians**. Not just an optician she also dispensed drugs, wines and toilet requisites ... a combination which would not go together well in this day and age. This opticians was in service in the 1920s and was situated approximately where the **Mecca Bingo**, once the **Ritz Cinema**, now stands. **Frederick William Pittuck** opened his premises here at number 93 by 1911. He was a dispensing chemist at Hebburn in 1875 and at Newcastle in 1895 in partnership with J.C. Snowden. **Miss Pittuck** was operating her optician shop from this location between 1927-1937.

John Lewis Holmes & Son

John Lewis Holmes & Son were saddlers who later became ironmongers about 1909. Morley M. Holmes moved the business to 91 High Street West and it operated from here from 1911-1929. Located by the archway near the Black Bull was **Richardson's** the butchers. One of the employees of this shop, who was known to always wear a bow tie, was the owner of the first Mini in Wallsend.

Robert Anthony

At number 86 stood a jewellers shop called **Robert Anthony**.

F.W. Woolworth

Around 1930 **F.W. Woolworth** was in business at 73-76 High Street West. It was situated somewhere near where the entrance to the Forum now stands. It moved further down the High Street to the south corner of Station Road and High Street East in 1958. In 2009 **Woolworths** closed and **Well Worth It** started trading in its place, although this shop closed in 2010.

Watson's Leather Co

Watson's Leather Company, at number 65 was the second leather and hardware shop in close proximity with **A.W. McCullagh** who was mentioned earlier as being at number 132.

Tates Radio

Tates had a showroom selling radios and TVs at number 64-66.

Walter Willsons

A high quality grocers shop, **Walter Willsons** was situated at number 61 High Street West, having the telephone number 623459. This grocers store was founded in 1875 and according to its advert presented a warm 'smiling service'. Nowadays the site of this shop is roughly where the **Catalogue Shop** stands in the Forum. In the photograph right the name Walter Willson can just be seen on the right hand side and confirms the shop would have been just opposite where **Ethel Austin's** shop and the **Kentucky Fried Chicken** shop are today.

High Street, Wallsend.   (No. 117)

E. Hay

A high quality butcher shop located at 54 High Street West, **Edward Hay's** sold mainly sausages, cold meats, pies and sandwiches. Situated on the south side of the High Street, the shop was beside what is now **St Oswald's** shop. This butchers shop was renowned for selling quality goods. How many of us can remember polony, brawn, home rendered lard as well as the normal prime pork, pies and sausages that the butchers often sold.

London & Newcastle Tea Company
This was a grocery and Provisions shop located at 51 High Street West who gave stamps against purchases which could be exchanged for goods, a forerunner to Green Shield, as did **Thompson's Red Stamps Store.**

Timothy Whites and Taylors
At number 47 this chemist had been around for a long time. It was located on the north side opposite what are now **Chirton Fisheries** and **St Oswald's Hospice.**

Jas. Dickinson
Photographers **Jas. Dickinson** stood at number 43 but will be covered on page 64.

L&N Stores
This picture which was received from Don Price shows a few other shops which were located between the Black Bull and the Station Hotel including **Milburn's**, a tobacconist shop, **F. Robson & Co** and **L&N Stores.** These shops stood about where Barclays bank now stands. First was **F. Robson & Co.** Next to that was some sort of alleyway and then **Milburn's Newsagents and Stationers** who advertised "Bristol Filter Virginia" in bold letters above the shop entrance and a smaller sign on the wall advertised "Players". Next to this stood **L&N Stores** who proudly advertised their groceries' prices on the windows.

Welcut Tailors
This gent's outfitters may have been on High Street West.

Gladson's
Well known for having the half round upstairs window, which is still there to this day. This shop was later to become a branch of **Cornelius** the tailors shop (we will talk more about **Cornelius** later in the book) and may well now be beside **Maple Textiles** at number 42, which was established in 1975. **Gladson's** was known as a drapers, tailors and outfitters shop and was one of the shops who participated in the Provident scheme for payment of goods.

David Gillis
Furniture maker **David Gillis** stood at numbers 33/35/37 High Street West. Between what is now the **Mecca Bingo Hall** and Station Road on the north side of High Street West was a number of shops including **Middlemast, Milne, Slater, Davison, Ainsworth, Ruddicks** through to **Wilson's** which stood next to The Station Hotel.

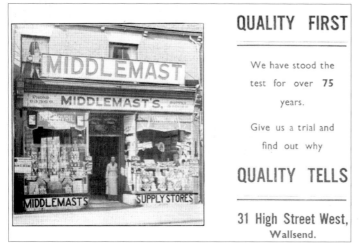

QUALITY FIRST

We have stood the test for over **75** years.

Give us a trial and find out why

QUALITY TELLS

31 High Street West,
Wallsend.

Middlemast
Edward **Middlemast**, a grocer, established his business at 31 High Street West about 1885. His son John Henry took over when Edward retired shortly before 1900 but John died in 1909 following an operation. He was a Liberal, a Freemason and a member of the Tradesmen's Association and the Heaton Camera Club. After 1909 the shop continued under Mrs Emily Middlemast. **Middlemast's** were succeeded by **Hadrian** grocers.

Milne

In 1905 **John Milne** opened his fruiterers shop near **Middlemast's** shop. There was also a John Milne's shop nearby trading as a saddler's, travelling draper and bookmaker but it is unknown if there was any connection between these two shops.

Hadrian Self-Service Grocery

Prior to the demolition of many shops to make way for the new **Forum Shopping Centre**, **Hadrian Self-Service Grocery**, a new idea in shopping, was located at number 31 High Street West. The **Hadrian Supply Company**, part of a chain developed from a corner shop, opened the first supermarket in the newly built Forum.

Ruddick's

Next door to **Hadrian**, **Ruddick's** greengrocers at 27-29, followed an older trader in the same line, **John Milne**, who was thought to have been on this site in 1905.

Workwear Suppliers

Next door to these stood **Workwear Suppliers**, whose predecessors had been **Slaters** and **Davison Pawnbrokers** shop and before that, **F. Murphy**, a draper and beer retailer.

Ainsworth's

Next door to this at number 21, were fishmongers, **Ainsworth's** around 1932 onwards. It was well known for having a fish sign hanging above the shop. In the 1920s before it became **Ainsworth's** it had been two shops, **Maynards** the confectioners and the **Danish Butter Company**, the latter being traceable back as far as the 1890s.

A. Anderson
A. Anderson was an established boot and shoe dealer located at 33 High Street West.

Watson the Butcher
Situated at number 22 High Street West, **Watson's** also had shops at Potter Street in Willington Quay and Ravensworth Street in Rosehill.

T. & G. Allan
This shop was located on High Street West and was part of the Forum Shopping Centre.

Greenwood's
This tailors shop has been established since around 1862 as shown on a sign above the door. It is located on the corner of High Street West and Atkinson Street. For those of

you with a keen eye who have seen the Likely Lads film which was partly shot in Wallsend, you may have noticed this shop in the background when Terry was driving his sales van along the High Street. (See also page 65.)

Next to these and just before the Station Hotel were the premises of **Carole's** ladies outfitters at the front and **Percy Carr's** hairdresser at the side, previously **Burlinson's**.

Before the Second World War, the front shop had been held by a succession of bakers, ending with **Miller's Hill** bakers. In a photo taken around the time of the Second World War there is a 'TUROG' sign above the front of this shop. The 'TUROG' sign has also been seen above the front of one of **Backley's** bakers shop so it is not known if one of the bakers who owned this shop before Miller's Hill was Backley's or not.

Robert L Blackburn was a confectioner at 122 High Street West, later becoming number 120 around 1910. **Blackburn Ltd** was later referred to as **Backley's (R.L. Blackburn) Ltd** by 1930 with William J. Backley having been the manager for a time previously.

Opposite these shops stood **John Ogden's Funeral Service**, which may have operated only a short time between 1910 and 1911.

Beside this stood the **Clyde Street Joinery** which was established in 1904.

Hepworth's
In the 1960s between the Station Hotel and **Martin's Bank** on High Street West near Station Road, stood **Hepworth's** seen here in the photograph on the right, it is the first shop on the left hand side.

Martin's Bank
Both **Martin's** and **Midland** had bank premises on the very beginning of High Street West. **Martin's** was on the north side approximately where the Market Woman statue and surrounding seating area is today and **Midland** was on the south side.

Midland Bank

This bank was located just to the west of what was **Burton's** shop and was most likely where the **Café on the Tyne** now stands.

Burton's Tailor Shop

Burton's gent's outfitting shop stood right on the corner of High Street West and Station Road. The rounded shape of the name above the window can still be seen today, although it is just painted black. This later became **Graftons** (see photo below) and is now **Greenways**.

Graftons

Seen here in this interesting photograph from around the early 1960s, **Graftons** clothes shop can clearly be seen on the left below the **Wallsend Memorial Hall**. Notice in the background the scaffolding around the **Wallsend Co-operative** store. This may be just being built which would probably date the photo at about 1966/67. It is also interesting to notice the junction with the old type traffic lights and the two boys on the bicycles. Photograph of **Graftons** supplied by Malcolm Dunn.

Wallsend Travel Agency

The **Wallsend Travel Agency** was situated at number 5 High Street West, a site now occupied by the Market Woman statue and seating area today.

The 'Green ...' Shops

In Wallsend there were over a period of years three shops all starting with the word 'Green' in the name of the shop. The first of these shops was Greenwell's shop which was a grocers located around where the Co-operative Funeral parlour is now but it was situated in the building prior to the present building which was built in 1924. The next shop is Greenwood's tailor shop which is still located at the corner of Atkinson Street and High Street West and was established in 1860. The last one is Greenways and is a grocery shop located at the corner of High Street West and Station Road, directly beneath the room used by the Wallsend Local History Society for their monthly meetings in the Memorial Hall.

Here are a few advert from businesses on High Street West.

During the Second World War

It was said that during the Second World War some of the shops on the south side of High Street West had the first floor rooms taken over by the Army to use as 'signing on' headquarters. The rooms, now mostly flats, were all made into one by having the connecting walls altered to give access through doorways to make one long room. This room apparently stretched near enough the whole length of the buildings from Portugal Place to Border Road (the flat above one of the arches having been occupied by the author's great aunt at one time).

At this point we finish with High Street West and start our journey along High Street East.

High Street East

We will begin with the south corner of High Street East and Station Road where for many years **Woolworths** plied its trade.

F.W. Woolworths

This store began in Wallsend on High Street West around 1930 and moved to its more recent location in 1958, replacing the old bill board notices on the gable end of the shop at the start of High Street East. **Woolworths** bragged that it sold "nothing over 6d" (2^1/$_2$p today). The site of this store was known at one time to have been named Swan Road. In 2009 **Woolworths** closed and **Well Worth It**, a family run business, took over in its place although this only had a short life and it closed in 2010.

The next few shops are located on the south side of High Street East between Woolworths and the Wallsend Social Club building, the ground floor premises of the club now being a hairdressing shop, **Eric's**.

Evening News

The **Evening News**, which is understood to have been the forerunner for the Evening Chronicle, used to operate from number 12 High Street East as advertised in the Wallsend Guide book of 1951. Also at one time this shop belonged to **William Atkinson**, who was described as an accomplished watchmaker. He ran this shop at number 12 High Street East between 1914 and 1929. After that the shop was taken over by **C. Bianchi** who traded as a gramophone dealer.

Lawson's Travel shop

Lawson's Travel shop also had a shop premises on Station Road. At one time, due to the fact that the local bus company did not have a canteen premises, it was possible to find some of the inspectors from the buses having a break in this shop. The company shop was taken over by Edmund Hall, Chairman of the Wallsend Local History Society, when he started to operate his own bus service in Wallsend and the local area.

Opposite **Lipton's** on the south side of High Street East, stood **John Richardson's** drapery shop which was established around 1902. John Richardson died on a train between Howdon and Wallsend around 1920. John Joseph Richardson held the shop until 1929 when it was later to become **Moore's Stores**.

Bon Marche

Many people have fond memories of this store. **Bon Marche** was started by Mrs Lily Anne Smith and was opened as a draper's shop on 7th March 1904. Because there was a shop next door to her new shop already called Smith's, she chose the name **Bon Marche**. She became so successful that in a short time her husband, Joseph, joined her. He had a draper shop on the opposite side of the High Street, next to his mother-in-law, Mrs Elizabeth Pile, who had a butchers shop. Mrs Pile retired in 1955 and Joseph Smith, presumably her son-in-law, took over the business. In 1909 the shop premises moved slightly further down the street. Stanley Smith joined the firm in 1916. The building was extensively re-furbished and extended in 1936-37, when footwear, toys and furnishings were added to the shop trade. They opened a new shop in 1947 on the opposite side of the street, at number 21-31, which sold electrical appliances. It had a really good curtain department, as well as other departments. Children's wear and ladies wear were on the first floor and there was a lovely sweeping staircase up to the first floor. They also had a bakers and confectionery shop, where you could buy beautiful cakes. At Christmas they would open up a showroom especially as a toy fair.

The old photo right shows **Bon Marche** on the corner of Sycamore Street and High Street East and next door to this shop heading towards Station Road was **J. McDonald**. **Bon Marche** on the corner was at one time **Cornelius** the tailors and is now **Eric's** hairdressing salon.

S.J. Cornelius

The premises of Bon Marche were taken over by **S.J. Cornelius**, a tailor and clothier supplying all sorts of clothing for men and boys. **Cornelius** sold various draperies and it was also a very posh shoe shop. It had shops at numbers 16/18/19 High Street East. Number 16 was a ladies' tailor/clothier, number 18 was a boys' tailor/clothier and number 19 was a men's tailor/clothier. The railings around Sycamore Street toilets, which were more commonly known as 'Poet's Corner', were bought by Arnie Waugh of **Wallsend Motor Company** and relocated at his Forest Hall farm.

Opposite this shop on the eastern corner of Sycamore Street stood the **Army and Navy Store** which traded around the 1970s onwards. It is now **Blue Line Taxis**.

At this point we will cross over the road onto the north side of High Street East and back up to the junction with Station Road. In the late 1800s and the beginning of the 1900s this was the location of the Zion Chapel. This chapel was bought by Mr MacHarg and was demolished in 1902. The Allen Memorial Church on Park Road was built to replace it. In place of the Zion Chapel he built the magnificent **Central Buildings**. These were completed and opened in 1903 as depicted by the date stone which can still be seen at the top south face of the building.

Many shops were located in the Central Buildings and we will try to remember them. Some more shops are covered in the chapter 'North of the High Street'.

Probably the most famous name to have been trading from this building was **Boots the Chemist**. You can still see the name in the tiles at the foot of the doorway on the corner of the shop which is now **Classic Trends and Textiles** and a sign above the door advertises the shop as 106 Station Road.

Boots The Chemist
This photo was taken at the entrance to the old **Boots** store. Although this chemist shop is now long gone, the sign in the floor tiles still remain to this day.

Weir, Webb & Bourn
This was a well known estate agent and was trading from number 1 High Street East; between what was **Boots** on the corner of High Street East and Station Road, on the ground floor of the Central Buildings and Woodbine Avenue.

The following shops were trading around the end of the 1940s: **Carrick's Catering Ltd**, which at a later date changed the shop sign from **Carrick's Catering Ltd** to just simply **Carrick's**; **J. Dampney and Co**, and **Fairbairns**, the shoe shop, who seems to have taken over the premises which were once **Liptons**.

At number 11 High Street East was **Launcelot Soulsby** who was a draper and milliner from Blyth. This shop was later to become a branch of **Liptons** between 1909 and 1929. After that it became **George Hill and Sons** stationers shop, a company established in 1901.

At number 17 High Street East and Woodbine Avenue at the beginning of the 1900s was **Smithson's Wallpaper Shop**. It was opened around April 1902 with the advertising slogan "famous dealer in paper-hangings-no firm in England can sell wallpaper cheaper!" A few years later it became **Sanderson and Co**, a furnishing ironmongers from Blyth. It had also been a local firm called **Foster & Hornsby**, cabinet makers. It may also have been **Mrs Curry's Albion Café** and in 1909, **Adam Tomlinson's** shoe shop. From 1910 onwards it was the **Public Benefit Boot Company Limited** and this company may have run for many years. These would have been where the **Newcastle Building Society** and the **William Hill** betting shop stand today.

Around 1916 the **National Egg Market** stood at the eastern corner of Woodbine Avenue on High Street East.

Bon Marche Ltd
The photo on the left shows the location of the newer of the **Bon Marche** shops which was located on the north side of High Street East from numbers 21-31. This impressive shop took over from the one which was located on the corner of Sycamore Street, below the Wallsend Social Club. It is now the location of **Jet Amusements** and **Thompson Opticians** and was once **Age Concern** and **Mega Pound World**.

W. & T. Pearce

This plumbers shop at number 24 appeared in the 1951 Guide to Wallsend and was located on the south side of the High Street. Today the shop is trading as **Fotosnaps**.

R. Brown

Opposite the above shop on the north side of the High Street at number 25 stood a footwear shop which traded under the name of **R. Brown** in and around 1908. At some time the premises would have been incorporated in the **Bon Marche** building.

Jeavons

At number 26 stood **Jeavons** record player and accessory shop. It advertised the sale of all the latest 'pop' recordings and 'a record service second to none'.

HOURS OF PLEASURE
FOR YOUR LEISURE !

ALL THE LATEST 'POP' RECORDINGS

STEREOPHONIC, LONG PLAY, EXTENDED PLAY, PROGRESSIVE AND TRADITIONAL JAZZ, CLASSICAL, ETC.

RECORD SERVICE SECOND TO NONE

RECORD PLAYERS, RECORD CASES, TAPE RECORDERS AND ACCESSORIES.

Large Selection of GUITARS (including all Hofner Models), STRINGS, CORDS, MACHINE HEADS. etc.

PIANO ACCORDIONS AND MOUTH ORGANS

LEADING AGENTS FOR GRUNDIG TAPE RECORDERS AND ALL ACCESSORIES.

REPAIRS—Qualified "Grundig Trained" Engineer Available.

THERE'S A "SOUND" CHOICE AT

JEAVONS for RECORDS
26, HIGH STREET EAST, WALLSEND

Kay's

Around the late 1950s, trading at number 30, stood **Kay's** drapers and outfitters.

Clarke's

Around 1908 stood **Clarke's** the well known pastry cook and confectioners, trading on the north side at number 33.

T.O. Marshall

At number 33-35 stood **T.O. Marshall's** chemist shop as advertised in the 1951 Wallsend Guide book. This chemist presumably took over the premises from **Clarke's** confectioners.

J.T. Branley

Opposite the above shop on the south side of the High Street at number 34 stood **J.T. Branley's** grocery and provisions shop.

Rediffusion

Rediffusion traded from number 34a. It was a television showroom and was advertised in the 1951 guide book.

A. Cornelius

Between the years 1910 and 1935, drapers and outfitters **A. Cornelius** traded at number 41 High Street East. It also offered the latest in the line of millinery. Presumably **A. Cornelius** was in some way connected with **S.J. Cornelius** who traded further up High Street East on the corner of Sycamore Street.

Direct Supplies

The 1951 Guide book shows that there was a work wear and outdoor wear shop named **Direct Supplies** trading at number 41 High Street East. The proprietor of this shop, which was advertised in the 1901-1951 Wallsend Jubilee booklet, was a Mr I. Gould. They supplied everything for the outdoor person including the 'worker, camper, hiker and cyclist'.

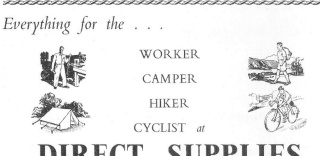

Everything for the . . .

WORKER

CAMPER

HIKER

CYCLIST *at*

DIRECT SUPPLIES

41 HIGH STREET EAST - WALLSEND-ON-TYNE

(Proprietor : I. GOULD)   (Telephone : Wallsend 63368)

William Pile

William Pile was trading as a butcher at number 42-44 High Street East as advertised in the 1951 guide book. He was a 'family butcher and contractor' giving a high class of 'service and satisfaction to all areas'. In the booklet it is said that he had been established for 46 years.

Industrial, Trades and Civic Exhibition

In the Jubilee year of 1951, Wallsend held an exhibition on the Green from 9th to 16th June 1951. Many local companies held stalls in this exhibition including **George Hill & Son** (Wallsend) Ltd, Merchants, Factors and Importers, 11 & 13 High Street East, and advertised as giving 'fifty years of service in Ironmongery, Stationery, Newsagents, Sports Goods, Hardware, Cutlery, Tools, Tobacco, Seeds and all Garden Requisites, Builders Merchants, Toys and Games.'

Trustee Savings Bank

The Wallsend Branch of the **Trustee Savings Bank** is still in the same place, on the south side of High Street East, on the site of the building which was where the **Regal** Picture House stood, on the opposite side of the High Street to the Brunswick Church. It is now known as Lloyd's TSB – the sign of the black horse. There was also a branch of the **Trustee Savings Bank** on Tynemouth Road, Howdon, just a few doors west of **Brodie's** Store. This branch of **Lloyd's** has now closed and a cash dispenser is located at the building, adjacent to **The Vine Café.**

Levey's

Levey's wallpaper store stood at number 47 on the north side of the road. In more recent times the shop has now been taken over by '**Go-As-You-Please**' undertakers who previously traded from the corner of Park Road before moving to this site.

Dudley Charlton

Estate agents **Dudley Charlton** used number 51 as one of their many sites for their shops.

R.W. Stokoe

At one time a specialised shop trading in the fruit business was **R.W. Stokoe**. On the front of his shop he advertised as 'The Wallsend Fruit and Nut Centre.' At a later date the shop was better known as **John Sibley Pets** shop and is now **Go-As-You-Please** funeral services.

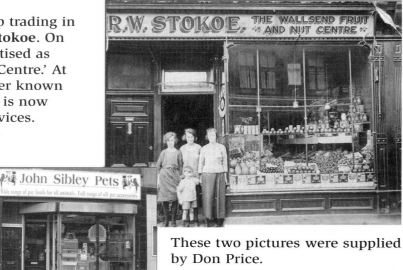

Disque Records

Around the 1980s/1990s at 55 High Street East was a record shop named **Disque Records**. It was run by Joan and Terry Utterson, who specialised in 'golden oldies' having a range of nostalgic songs from the 1950s, 60s and 70s. They also sold many instruments such as violins, guitars and recorders.

These two pictures were supplied by Don Price.

Arthur Bell

At 48a-52 stood **Arthur Bell** who advertised his shop as a 'Florist and High Class Fruiterer' selling choice flowers, fruit and vegetables daily and specializing in 'floral tributes of all kinds'. Today this site is occupied by another local fruit shop, **Tom Owen's** and also solicitors **Smith – Corsey**.

R. Calvert

Established in 1888, **R. Calvert's** was a family butcher who traded at number 54 and 56 and proudly boasted of 'always giving the best quality'.

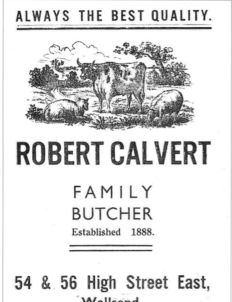

ALWAYS THE BEST QUALITY.

ROBERT CALVERT

FAMILY BUTCHER

Established 1888.

54 & 56 High Street East, Wallsend.

John McCreesh's

Around 1908 **John McCreesh** was trading in his hardware shop at number 60 High Street East supplying such things as ironmongery, mantles, glass, china and earthen ware 'to make your home bright and cheerful'.

Robert Harrison's

At the corner of Park Road and High Street East stood **Robert Harrison's** shoemaking shop. Mr Harrison ran shops at both ends of Wallsend High Street; his first shop at 57 High Street operating from around 1890. He was the son of another boot manufacturer, his father being John Harrison. Robert married Edith Calvert in 1887 at Willington Quay. Edith died in 1894. Robert ran his shops until he died in 1920 and he was succeeded by Mrs Margaret Harrison. He may have been the first occupant of this shop between about 1901-13. The shop was taken over by **Barclays Bank** until 1974. The 'eagle' sign of **Barclays Bank** above the door could still be seen until newly opened estate agents called **Mike Rogersons** covered the sign up.

Braidford's

On the opposite side of Park Road stood the **Borough Theatre**. It opened in 1908 and was demolished in 2011. We will cover this building in more detail in a later chapter. These buildings also contained **Braidford's Music and Record Shop**.

Backley's

This was one of several bakeries owned by **Backley's**.

R.L. Blackburn Ltd

R.L. Blackburn Limited was a high class confectioner and the address given is 62 and 64 High Street East. It was described as a first class firm supplying the finest quality confectionery. One of the directors of this company was a Mr S.P. Borella and the other being B.J. Borella.

Moffett's

Moffett's Supply Stores was known as a 'tea dealer and coffee roaster' as well as being a supplier of home fed bacon and best flour. They also had a shop on Chillingham Road, Newcastle.

Hamill School of Dancing

Next door to the Borough at number 75 stood the **Hamill School of Dancing**. Two of the principals of this dance school were Alf and Rose Hamill. Both were accomplished dancers, especially Alf who had numerous letters after his name, and taught almost any kind of dance including modern ballroom, Latin American, tap dancing and old time dancing. Their studio adjoined the Borough and the ground floor later became a hair dressing shop, the **Hair Salon**, which closed in 2009/10.

The HAMILL School of Dancing
75 High Street East, Wallsend-on-Tyne
(Adjoining Gaumont Theatre)

PRINCIPAL :
Alf. Hamill
Past President, Fellow and Examiner of the Northern Counties Dance Teachers' Association (Ballroom and Latin-American Branches).
Fellow N.A.T.D. (Ballroom).
Fellow I.D.M.A. (Ballroom).
Fellow (Comm.) M.A.T.D. (Ballroom).
Member I.S.T.D. (inc.) (Ballroom).
Member (Comm.) I.D.M.A. (Latin-American).
Member (H.Comm.) N.C.D.T.A. (Old Time)
Fellow F.I.D. (Paris).
General Secretary and Treasurer N.C.D.T.A.

PRINCIPAL :
Rose Hamill
Member (H.Comm.) N.C.D.T.A. (Old-Time.)
Associate (Comm.) I.D.M.A. (Ballroom).
Associate N.A.T.D. (Ballroom).

Veronica Hamill
Member N.C.D.T.A. (Stage).
Associate I.D.M.A. (Tap).

MODERN BALLROOM, LATIN-AMERICAN, OLD TIME and TAP DANCING.

Jewitt's

Moving down the High Street to the east of Park Road at number 76 on the south side stood **Fred Jewitt's** shop. The Jewitt family were well known in Wallsend having started off with Anthony Jewitt who owned a butcher shop at 45 Benton Way. There was also a Mark Jewitt at Buddle Street. Mrs Mary Jewitt took over the business from Anthony sometime before 1901. Mark Albert Jewitt died in 1907 and his business seems to have been taken over by his wife, Lucy.

By 1924 Frederick Jewitt had set up his shop and his home address was Cross House Villa on Wallsend Green. Fred Jewitt was a well known swimmer and was regularly seen at Wallsend baths, diving off the boards on a Sunday morning. Because of this he is presumably the same Fred Jewitt who joined the Wallsend Amateur Swimming Club when it started in 1912. He was the President of this swimming club when he officiated at the Helsinki Olympic Games in 1952.

Mark Jewitt is known to have started his own shop at 84 Park Road in the 1930s. The premises at 76 are now next to **Soprano's Italian Restaurant** which is at numbers 78-80.

Henry Keedy

Another fresh fish shop and a poultry dealer was **Henry Keedy** who traded at number 78 around 1908 before Ainsworth took over the shop.

Ainsworth

Mr **Fred Ainsworth** had one shop on High Street West and this one at 78 High Street East as well as a shop in Byker. My father being a motor mechanic all of his life in Wallsend remembers Mr Ainsworth having had a Humber Super Snipe motor car. Fred Ainsworth worked with **Percy Garrod** between 1922 and 1931. A well known fishmonger in his own right Fred opened his own shop at 21 High Street West in 1932. Number 78 is now also part of **Soprano's Italian Restaurant**.

J.J. Duds

Another butchers shop, this one **Mr J.J. Duds** stood at 78 High Street East. He was known as an English pork butcher and kept his shop spotlessly clean.

Neeb – (Electricity Service Centre)

The **North Eastern Electricity Board** operated from number 80 through the **Local Electricity Service Centre**.

Gwen Jones

At number 82 was **Gwen Jones** who specialised in male and female underwear, especially 'Sparwick ladies underwear' and 'Men's Oak Tree underwear'.

The Modern Carpet Company

These floor covering specialists, **The Modern Carpet Company**, were advertised in the 1962 Wallsend Guide booklet informing 'advice freely given by experts' and were located at number 82.

Raymond Swan

This shop is still in the same place on the south side of High Street East, although it has long since been closed. The shop facia was painted a dark blue. Just visible on the top of the shop window is part of the shop's logo: 'The Firm Founded on Friendship', although most of it is covered by the metal roller shutter which has been installed. It is located opposite and just down from the Coronation Club. **Raymond Swan** stood at number 94 and was a well known television and radio dealership.

Moore's

At number 98 around the 1980s and 90s was a food store called **Moore's**. They sold all sorts of ingredients for cake making in their own competitively priced scooped food range. It was owned by Mrs Moira Moore and offered a general dealers 'small shop' atmosphere. They also stocked tinned foods and dairy products.

Dodds Brothers

Dodds Brothers, who sold wireless gramophones and records, used to have a shop at 114 High Street East. It was also advertised as an Exide Service Station. Exide was the maker of batteries. They used to deliver in a weird contraption which seems to have been part motor-cycle and part wagon. It may have been a three-wheeled vehicle. Photo supplied by Don Price (original by Olive Broad).

Joseph Harbit

In 1908 **Joseph Harbit** was recognised as one of the oldest established butchers trading at number 119.

Arthur Tinkler

At number 126 was **Arthur Tinkler's** shop. It was described as a 'bespoke Tailors, Men's and Boys Clothiers and Outfitters' and was one of the shops which participated in the Provident Company scheme accepting Provident Checks as a payment system.

P.R. Garrod

P.R. Garrod's was a local butcher where my aunt Audrey Boundey used to work. Situated at number 130 on the south side it is now **Norman Taylor Photographer** and **Furniture Link**. Fred Ainsworth used to be one of his employees before he set up on his own. The firm was begun by Edward Albert Garrod at 130 High Street East around 1910. In 1921-22 the shop was taken over by Percy Robert Martin Garrod who was thought to have been Edward's son. Percy opened a new shop soon after at 108 High Street West.

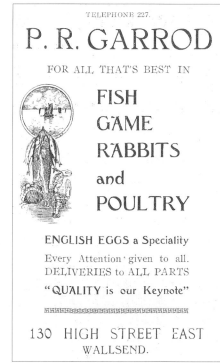

London & Newcastle Tea Company

This company had one business on 51 High Street West and another at 142 High Street East.
The premises at 142 are now **Tynecastle Carpets**.

J & R Millar

At this point I am unsure what sort of shop **J & R Millar's** was but it can be seen in this picture which was taken around 1968 that features the Royal Engineers Pipe Band leading the Remembrance Day Parade of that year. The building is now known as **Motorworld**.
(Photo supplied by Don Price. Original supplied by D. Cartwright.)

Tru-Time Taxis

This taxi firm was located at 134 High Street East, and was run by Ray Bolt who advertised in the 1946 issue of the Town's People magazine. They boasted that 'Weddings a Speciality' and 'distance was no object'.

Garland & Company

A taxi company and an undertakers, **Garland & Company** used to transport people around whether they were alive or not. They were located at number 146, which is opposite **Motorworld**.

R.E. Moore

At number 149 stood **R.E. Moore** who was a painter, decorator and sign writer, who boasted that he 'would undertake all Church and House decoration', and sold all decorating materials at a cheap price.

J. High

At number 151 in around 1908, was another 'High Class Fruiterer and Florist', **J High**. They also specialised in making wreaths and crosses. My relatives down the line were also the High family. It may have been one of these who owned this shop or not, but a relative of mine did own a shop on the High Street, believed to have been on the corner of Park Road and High Street. John High was a captain of a minesweeper who lost his life in the First World War and is buried in Church Bank Cemetery.

Hilda Birkett

Hilda Birkett was a ladies' hairdresser and advertised as being 'open every day' including 'late night Friday'.

John Day

Next door to **Hilda Birkett's** stood **John Day's** fruit and vegetable shop. John Day also has a shop on High Street West and is still trading in 2011. **Day's** arranged potatoes in a large box with a hole in the bottom so that he could scoop out measures of potatoes and place them straight into a customer's bag.

M.E. Bennett

Bennett's, at number 159, was a milliners shop around 1925. The shop was later taken over by **Fletcher James**, the well known estate agents operating from this site around 1950s who also had a shop on Station Road opposite the Forum, at a much later date. Number 159 is now occupied by **Dream Hair** hairdressers.

T. Pringle

At number 165 was **T. Pringle's** bakery and confectionery shop which was trading around the 1940s.

Ruddick's

Opposite these few shops, on the south side, was another fruit shop, **Ruddick's** where my mother, Elsie Boundey used to work.

Aquarius Boutique

This boutique, located at number 166, advertised in the 1972-1973 edition of the Wallsend Guide booklet. Unfortunately there is no information to say what kind of boutique it was.

Cash & Exchange

At number 167 stood the **Cash and Exchange** shop which was described as a 'Jewellery and Gift Specialist' and advertised in the Wallsend 'Townspeople's Bulletin' September to October 1946 issue. Very similar to a pawn shop it also advertised a 'Christmas Club'.

Marcel

At number 169 stood **Marcel's**, a specialist costume shop which traded around 1925. Its location today is the car park on the north side of High Street East between Alexander Street and Northumberland Street, just south of the Wallsend Police Station and Station Houses.

Giles

At number 182 stood **Giles** high class grocery and provisions shop. Giles also had a shop at number 111 High Street West. The photograph above is a Giles shop on High Street East beside the Central Buildings and seems to be of another shop owned by Giles which stood somewhere around 3-17 High Street East.

L.J. Winters

From 1921 onwards Joseph Winters had a number of grocery stores at 3, 86 and 182 High Street East. Joseph lived in Grange Villas, Wallsend. Leonard J. Winters who lived at the same address is known to have managed these shops until the early 1930s when he moved to Newcastle. L.J. Winters ceased trading in 1931.

Proctor

Just down from **Giles** was **Proctor's** shop which was trading around the mid 1950s.

Duncan

This shop stood on the south side near where the pedestrian crossing is now. **Duncan's** was thought to have been a grocers shop.

T.R. Boon

Boon's was described as 'a really traditional family chemists shop' with a very high counter, lots of mahogany wood drawers and sparkling glass. Delivery of all the medicines was taken in bulk and then put up in papers and bottles for the customers when they came in. Staff used to roll their own pills and make all sorts of bottles. The site where **Boon's** stood, number 186 High Street East, is now **Toddle In** baby wear shop. It may be noted that **Boon's** worked all days of the week, most days 11 hours a day from 9 am until 8 pm. They also worked for just 1 hour on a Sunday from 12 pm until 1 pm. In its advert in the 1962-1963 Wallsend Guide booklet it states 'This business now established for over half a century still maintains its original character of a traditional family chemist and druggist'. My father remembers that he used to work on Mr Boon's and his daughter's car, an Austin Princess 1100. The daughter married the vicar of St Peter's Church and they later moved away.

R. Craw

R. Craw's shop was known to have existed two doors down from **Boon's** in the mid 1950s. It is seen in a Pathe news clip which shows the visit by Queen Elizabeth II to Wallsend Town Hall on 4th November 1954. It is not known if this is part of the Craw family who owned a butcher shop in the early 1900s.

Metropolitan

Moving further down the High Street on the corner of Lawson Street stood the **Metropolitan Estate Agents**. This stood opposite the Town Hall and Municipal Buildings which were built in 1908.

A. Briggs

At number 203, which stood opposite the Town Hall on the north side stood, **A. Briggs**, a 'high class boot and shoe maker and repairer'. This business was going strong in and around 1925 and advertised with the slogan 'If your boots are worth repairing they are worth repairing well …' This is now the location of **Wallsend Taxis**.

Robert H.S. Craw

At number 204 High Street East, which is near the Town Hall, from 1909 until 1913 was a butchers shop belonging to **Robert Henry Stroud Craw**. Robert was conscripted into the Army in early 1918 as Private 45288 Robert Henry Stroud Craw of the 7th Service Battalion of the South Staffordshire Regiment and tragically was killed in action on 1st September 1918. Robert was also known to have stables on the site of the Coronation Club where he kept, amongst other animals, Irish cobs. His family had given up the shop after his death in 1918. It was taken over by **Mrs E. Bryson** and later became a part of the **Co-operative Society**. In the windows above his shop there were signs for **J.W. Wilson**, a printer and dry-salter. Next door at 202 High Street East was at one time owned by **Mrs E. Wilson** but it is unknown if they were related.

G.H. Parr

Well known watchmaker and jeweller, **G.H. Parr** was trading at number 209-211. They advertised in the 1951 Wallsend Jubilee booklet as being 'Wallsend's oldest established watchmaker' and 'repairers of watches, clocks, jewellery and spectacles'. It is now the location of **Angeltek Services**.

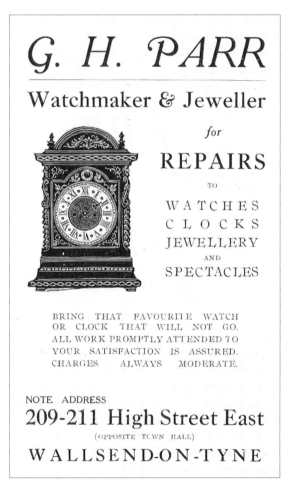

G. H. PARR

Watchmaker & Jeweller

for

REPAIRS

TO

WATCHES

CLOCKS

JEWELLERY

AND

SPECTACLES

BRING THAT FAVOURITE WATCH OR CLOCK THAT WILL NOT GO. ALL WORK PROMPTLY ATTENDED TO YOUR SATISFACTION IS ASSURED. CHARGES ALWAYS MODERATE.

NOTE ADDRESS

209-211 High Street East

(OPPOSITE TOWN HALL)

WALLSEND-ON-TYNE

R. Whitfield

Promising a 'prompt delivery to all parts', **R. Whitfield's** stood at number 224.

He was a high class grocer and a butcher and specialised in Danish bacon and butter. The advert for the shop can still be seen painted on the side of the building where he was located. It reads 'This is Whitfields the bacon specialist'.

T. Frazer

Newsagents and stationers, **T. Frazer** stood at number 227 and 229. Not only did he sell confectionery and tobacco he also an agent for Capern's bird food.

Peacock's

At number 248 was a butchers shop called **Peacock's**, famous for its beef and kidney pies. It was advertised in the Wallsend Jubilee Celebrations programme of June 1951.

Athey's Stores

Athey's Stores was a grocers shop trading around 1925 at number 270. Today it is owned by **Danials** and is a newsagents shop.

Joseph Robson

At the corner of Boyd Road and High Street East, just opposite the Richardson Dees School, was once a fine farm owned by **Joseph Robson**.

This photograph, taken from the archives of the Wallsend Local History Society, shows the farm as also trading as a Haulage Contractor, a furniture remover and coal merchant.

Photograph supplied by Don Price – Robson's Farm, East Farm cottage High Street East, Wallsend which was demolished 1934.

Wallsend Motor Company Ltd

In 1925 the **Wallsend Motor Company Limited** advertised many services. It stood on the waste ground beside the New Winning public house, what is now part of the Burnside Technical College grounds. Mainly a garage it offered Victory Chars-a-bancs (presumably long, bus-like vehicles which later gained the name Charabancs) which run on pneumatic tyres and catered for parties and tours of 'any distance'. It also advertised as a haulage contractor undertaking any class of work.

This is more than likely the fore-runner to the **Wallsend Motor Company** of which my father, Bill Boundey, was a long serving motor-mechanic, gaining a reputation for being a first class motor-mechanic. He remembers that one of the lads who used to work at this garage, Ronnie (surname unknown), left this job to become the first Traffic Warden in Wallsend.

Northumbrian Garage

The **Northumbrian Garage**, a sales and service garage, operated from High Street East and it was believed to be in the location of the New Winning pub. It may be the garage which was opposite the pub before becoming **Taylors Garage**, which is now the **ATS Garage** at the top of the Wagon Way. Bill Boundey remembers that Billy Mays took this garage over from **Taylors**. Billy Mays was described as a big lad who emigrated to Australia and the garage just disappeared after that.

The Firm Founded on Friendship

for

AND RADIO

**94, HIGH STREET EAST
WALLSEND**

PHONE: 623593

Above are adverts for shops on High Street East.

The next two shops have been kept to the last for a specific reason.

S.G. Anderson
Advertised only as being on High Street East, the exact location is unknown. **S.G. Anderson** was a shipping and family butcher who was trading around 1908, selling all types of meat. He was also known to send meat to any part of the district every day, although how far the 'district' covered is not known.

H. Thomson
Our last port of call in this section is **H. Thomson** who was a fish, game and poultry dealer again around 1908. This was another shop owner who only gave out the fact that he was located on High Street East and did not give any number so its exact location is not known. It is noticed in his advert that 'Ducks and Chickens killed to order'. Imagine the uproar if a butcher today boasted of this service!

North of the High Street

The next chapter takes us to the shops situated north of the High Street, following the area from west to east, although in some cases they may not be in exact order. We will start in the area of West Street.

Tompkins & Stubbs

Owned by Mr D.E. Tompkins, **Tompkins & Stubbs** was an electrical engineer and contracting firm at number 43 West Street. Giving free estimates they specialised in industrial and domestic installations.

J. Hickleton

Advertised in the 1951 Wallsend Jubilee booklet as a general drapers, **J. Hickleton** was located at number 47 West Street.

Lamond & Himson

Ladies and gents hairdressing shop **Lamond & Himson** were located at number 49 West Street and they also had a shop at 2 Atkinson Street. They were experts in all kinds of the latest methods of hair styling.

J. & W.O. Brown

Around the mid 1920s **J. & W.O. Brown** were pawnbrokers and owned a shop at number 1 Birkett Street. Birkett Street, which was situated at the back of the **Ritz Cinema**, was on the north side of High Street West, running north to south and would have joined the High Street approximately just opposite the Queens Head public house. It was demolished to make way for newer housing between the Duke of York public house and what is now the **Co-operative Funeral Service**, York Drive.

We now leave Birkett Street and move onto Hedley Street.

A.F. French

Around 1908 painter, paperhanger and decorator, **A.F. French** was located at number 7-9 Hedley Street, now long gone but which ran at a right angle from High Street West to Elton Street West.

Jennie Dunn

At some date before 1925, part of French's shop, number 9 Hedley Street, was **Jennie Dunn's** millinery shop. She also supplied 'fancy draperies of every description'.

T.F. & M. Trotter

This hairdressing business was located next door to Jennie Dunn's at number 11 & 11a about the same time in 1925 and was a well known ladies' and gentlemen's hairdressing and shampooing shop. They offered a specialist range of treatments from 'electric face and scalp massage' to 'high frequency violet ray treatment'. **Trotter** also had premises on Station Road. Around 1986 Trotter's were still trading as a hairdresser's for both men and women but were by then located at number 74 Station Road. In 1986 it was run by new manager, Yvonne Bruce.

J. Newell

At number 14 in and around 1925 stood meat purveyor **J. Newell**. He advertised about selling the 'best quality beef, mutton, pork, veal and lamb, (when in season)' describing his shop as the '**Hedley Street Meat Mart**' and in his advert he carried a picture of his horse and cart proudly displaying his name on the side of the cart, with the heading 'A Post card Brings Our Cart To Your Door'.

J. NEWELL

Meat Purveyor

For Best Quality Beef and Mutton, Pork, Veal and Lamb (when in season) Sausages a Speciality

ALL ORDERS PROMPTLY ATTENDED TO.
A Post Card brings our Cart to your door

Hedley Street Meat Mart
14 Hedley Street, Wallsend

R. Stone

Around the same time Newell's were trading, at number 19 was grocer and general dealers **R. Stone** who sold only 'the best and purest at lowest prices' and 'specialised in Green Fruit'.

George Gray

From around 1910 until 1935 butcher **George Gray** was located at number 39 Hedley Street. In his advert in the King's Silver Jubilee issue booklet of 1935, he used an excellent little poem to advertise his goods: "For meat George Gray cannot be beat, His baby beef is a treat, His Canterbury Lamb it is delicious, Sweet, tender and nutritious."

J. Ogston

Leaving Hedley Street we now move to Elton Street West where we find **J. Ogston**, a joiner at number 29 around 1908.

IF its Lighting or Electricity Consult

G. W. DODDS & Co.

Electrical Contractors
Lighting and Power Engineers

ELECTRIC BELLS AND 'PHONES SUPPLIED AND OVERHAULED

WIRELESS ACCESSORIES of any make and price supplied

:: We are Specialists in ::
Motor Car Lighting Sets

Promptest Attention given to all work entrusted

1 North Road, Wallsend

Co-op Garment Cleaning

Part of the **Co-operative Laundries Society**, this branch was located on Equitable Street which is just off West Street. The **Co-op Garment Cleaning** store offered cleaning from 5/- (5 shillings) and Dyeing from 9/6 (9 shillings and sixpence).

G.W. Dodds & Co

G.W. Dodds & Company were electrical contractors based at number 1 North Road around the mid 1920s.

Hollings' Garage

Located at 57 North Road was **Hollings' Garage** and engineering works who advertised in the King's Silver Jubilee issue of 1935 that they were the 'Morris Dealers of Wallsend'.

John Rochester & Sons

John Rochester and Sons was a blacksmith located in Clyde Street which was demolished to make way for the new shopping centre around 1963. It was one of the last four shops in that area and had been offered a move to Hadrian Road but they refused.

E. Findlay

Edward Findlay worked as a painter, sign-writer and decorator at Shields Road, Byker, before moving to 56 Clyde Street in 1936. It was located next to an old blacksmith's shop, **Rochester's**. Edward **Findlay's** business was later a paint shop taken over by Tom and Robson Findlay. A previous occupier of this shop may have been George Oates junior, a builder. **Findlay** also had a shop at 147 High Street West.

We now move on to Station Road.

Thornton Printers

Thornton Printers were located in the Central Buildings on Station Road at the junction with High Street East and West. They advertised in the Wallsend Guide book of 1925 and were established in 1893.

T. Rowntree

Also around the mid 1920s, **T. Rowntree's** was a fruit and potato merchant located at 108 Station Road who also owned a shop at 61 Carville Road.

Hatfields Pet Stores

Pet food suppliers **Hatfields Pet Stores** was located at number 134 and were trading around the 1950s and specialised in dog, bird and poultry food.

Jackdaw Café

Between 1935 and 1950 the **Jackdaw Cafe** was located on Station Road, the precise location is not known. It advertised in the Ritz Cinema 15th Birthday Week booklet (1935-1950).

Northern Gas Showrooms

On the eastern side of Station Road below what is now the Gym, where the wall is rounded, was the **Northern Gas Showrooms**. They advertised in the Wallsend Jubilee Guide 1901-51 with the slogan 'and now the modern trend ... Gas – always at your service'.

Bonnie Bairns

In 1986 **Bonnie Bairns** baby wear shop at 78 Station Road advertised their shop which sold nursery equipment, bouncing cradles and high chairs along with a lively selection of children and baby clothes.

Rhythm Records

The record shop, **Rhythm Records**, on the east side of Station Road at number 130, was taken over by Barbara Graham, sister-in-law of the author, in the early 1990s. Although it was a small shop, due to the fact that it had a shared doorway with the bicycle shop, **Tompkins** next door, it had a fantastic assortment of records and CDs. In 2009 these premises were located close by **L & J's Hairdressing** shop and the **Sunlight Laundry**. Above the Laundry shop used to be an old sign which has now been taken away or covered up. The sign used to read 'Best Clothing Alterations & Bridal Wear'. It is not known exactly which shop this advertised.

Mayfair Jewellers

At number 138 stood **Mayfair Jewellers**. It has been trading for many years in the more recent years but since 2009 it has been taken over by **Jewellery By Design**.

Fletcher James

Trading in Wallsend from around the 1950s, estate agents **Fletcher James** had a few premises with this one being beside number 138. It has more recently been taken over by another estate agent, **Next To Buy**.

Mantrea

Another long trading business of recent years and still going strong is hairdresser **Mantrea** at number 140-42 taking over at some date from where **Joyce Elliot** used to be located.

Joyce Elliot

This hair stylist, which was located at 142 Station Road, was one of the shops to celebrate the Centenary of St Luke's Church in the 1987 edition of the News Guardian.

Thomas Hedderly

Originally from Bath, plumber William Hedderly came to Wallsend in the 1830s and by 1836 he had established his business. In the 1850s he was described as a brazier and tinplate worker and sub-postmaster, becoming tinsmith and plumber by 1861. In the 1870s his wife, Margaret, continued the business in his name, becoming his widow by 1881. Around 1848 William's son **Thomas Hedderly** was born. The photograph above of **Hedderly's** was dated 2nd April 1963 and was before the development of Wallsend Forum. It shows the workshop at Swan Street, which was later to become Station Road at numbers 155/7/9, becoming their only premises after 1900. Their first business was located in High Street West around 1890. Richard Rutherford Hedderly was also a well-known plumber in Wallsend and is presumed to be related to these Hedderly's.

The Miners' Club

This club on the west side of Station Road was built in 1925 and was originally called the 'Wallsend G And Rising Sun Collieries Welfare Institute'.

Booze Busters

On the corner of Station road and North Street stands **Booze Busters**, which previously to this was **Victoria Wines**. Before that it was **Blenkinsops** who sold cigars and cigarettes with the smell of the cigars hitting you as you walked in the door.

Porter's

This newsagent's shop, which stands opposite the old Buddle School, was at one time owned by a Harold Cummings. It was taken over from him by an unknown person from Gosforth before being owned by Tommy and Mary Rantoul, a local pitman and then by Mark Rantoul, presumably a relative of the former owners. It is now owned by Shaun Porter.

Boons

At number 261 Station Road was **Boons** the chemist. This chemist was believed to be the daughter of **T.R. Boon** who had a chemist shop on High Street East. She moved from Station Road to the High Street to take over her father's shop. The premises today are a vet's surgery.

The Western Dairies

Although their main offices were on Forth Street in Newcastle, **Western Dairies** advertised their products in the Wallsend Jubilee Guide book of 1951 and listed six other premises, one of which was at number 287 Station Road.

Before leaving Station Road north, I would like to mention a few of the shops and businesses that have occupied the Central Buildings at the corner of Station Road and High Street East.

Thornton's Printers

John Thornton Printers Ltd was founded in November 1893 by John Thornton of Percy Main, who used to work at one time for the Newcastle Chronicle. He borrowed some money and rented a shop in Birkett Street. A few years later he leased premises in Central Buildings. The company grew in the 1920s and in 1928 they moved to larger premises in Sharpe Road. In 1934 a large fire destroyed the first floor of this building in Sharpe Road. In May 1970 they moved to larger premises once more which were once owned by the **Wallsend Industrial Co-operative Society**. **Wallsend Printing Works** were part of Thornton Printers Ltd.

> ## THE WEDDING.   SILVER PRINTING.
>
> A large assortment of Invitation Cards and Circulars. Compliments Cards with envelopes to match, and Wedding Cake Boxes can be supplied same day as ordered.
>
> ## SEE OUR SAMPLES IN OUR OWN SHOWROOMS
> ### AT THE WORKS
> And you'll be happy ever after.
>
> ## JOHN THORNTON (PRINTERS) LTD.
> The Wallsend Printing Works, Sharpe Road.   Tel. Wallsend 63531.

Central Billiards Hall

In their advert in the 1935 King's Silver Jubilee programme, the **Central Billiards Hall** boasted of having 10 first class billiard tables which were the 'best in the district'. The Billiard rooms were managed by Edward MacHarg.

Nova Sign Company

The **Nova Sign Company** advertised in the 1962-1963 issue of the Wallsend Guide booklet as trading from the Central Buildings. They made signs for all purposes and it is known that they made one of the signs which used to hang outside the Rosehill Tavern on Churchill Street which advertised Double Diamond beer.

We now leave the north side of Station Road and move on to other shops north of the High Street.

Eric Bowran

Hall Farm, which was located on Kings Road, was the property of Dairyman **Eric Bowran**. He placed an advert in the 1951 issue of the Wallsend Guide. It informed that his was the fourth generation of his family to produce and deliver milk in the Borough of Wallsend, having begun the farm in the Parish of Willington.

E.A. Overton

Moving on to Grey Street stood decorator and sign-writer, **E.A. Overton**, located at number 9. He was advertised in the Wallsend Jubilee 1951 Guide as a 'Painter, Paper-Hanger and Sign-Writer specialising in Graining' and used 'Modern Decorative Schemes'.

W. Turner

At number 203 Park Road in and around 1925 stood local builder and contractor, **W. Turner**. Although the advert in the 1925 edition of the Guide to Wallsend was pretty basic it did show a photograph of a nice bungalow but it was possibly not from the Wallsend area.

Tudor Taxis

Around 1946, **Tudor Taxis** were said to be located at 57 Kings Road, a private house near the Coast Road. Advertising in the Town's People's Bulletin, September/October 1946 issue, the owner and proprietor, W. G Johnson, offered a day and night service providing 'Service, Civility and Satisfaction' with 'Weddings a Speciality' and also promised a 'prompt service'.

Monitor

At the top of Kings Road North stood **Monitor Engineering**. This factory was demolished in the summer of 2006 and Hunters Edge housing estate was built in its place.

J.H. McKean

At number 8 Charlotte Street in the early 1970s stood **J.H. McKean**, who specialised in providing everything for the handyman including such things as windows, doors, wardrobes and cupboards and expert advice on 'do-it-yourself tiling'.

Clarke Brothers

This company was another building firm but their private address was located at number 57 Woodbine Avenue. **Clarke Brothers** advertised in the 1925 issue of the Wallsend Guide book and described themselves as 'Local Ex-Service Men' presumably serving their time in the forces during the First World War.

James Wilson

At some time trading at number 2a Richardson Street, was local window cleaner, **James Wilson**. He boasted of six years experience and cleaned shop and house windows of any size charging 1 penny upwards according to size.

Joseph Mullen

This well known name once owned a stone mason's yard at the top of Church Bank. **Joseph Mullen** was in business around 1925. There is a street in Wallsend called Mullen Road and it is thought that this may have been named after this person. Although his works was on Church Bank, he lived at Fernwood, Willington-on-Tyne, now Rosehill. It is thought that these works were taken over by **Strettles Memorials** in 1952, which made gravestones and had a small holding at the top of Church Bank on the north side,

Keep the memory green with brighter thoughts of loved ones gone before by applying to

JOSEPH MULLEN,

For all kinds of
MEMORIALS IN STONE, MARBLE AND GRANITE. Also TABLETS IN BRONZE, BRASS AND MARBLE.

Erected in any part of the Country at Lowest Possible Prices.

Residence: "FERNWOOD," ROSEHILL-ON-TYNE.

Works: **Church Bank : WALLSEND.**

ESTABLISHED OVER 30 YEARS.

at the junction of Church Bank and St Peters Road; along with a shop in Heaton. Unfortunately, although established in 1946 and after many years of trading, **Strettles** was forced to close this site due to vandalism in recent years.

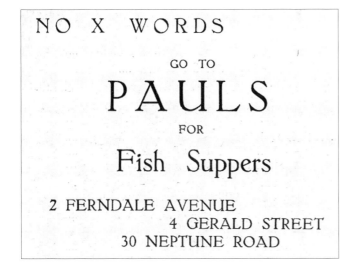

NO X WORDS

GO TO

PAULS

FOR

Fish Suppers

2 FERNDALE AVENUE
4 GERALD STREET
30 NEPTUNE ROAD

Paul's

In and around 1925 this fish and chips shop at number 2 Ferndale Avenue was one of many owned by **Paul's** in Wallsend. Along with this one, they had one at number 4 Gerald Street, which was on the site of what is now **Segedunum Roman Fort and Museum** and another at number 30 Neptune Road.

A.W. Hislop Ltd

Moving on to the Coast Road now. In and around the early 1960s **A.W. Hislop** used to be located on both sides of the Coast Road, around where the petrol station is now, next to the Rising Sun public house. They used to be called the **Blue Sign Service Stations** and were one of the places where my father, Bill Boundey, used to work. Previous to this the site was once **Hill's Garage**. Around 1946/47 whilst my father was working at **Hill's Garage** an Army Doctor dressed in full army uniform, turned up at the garage driving what was then a very expensive car, a Vauxhall 10. This doctor turned out to be Dr Cowper, who set up a practice in Howdon.

William Darling

Also on the Coast Road but thought to have been the north side just east of the Rising Sun public house, butcher **William Darling** would have been trading in and around the early 1900s. He advertised in the 1951 Jubilee issue of the Wallsend Guide book. With deliveries to all districts this butcher 'encouraged first class service and hygiene' in his shop.

P.L. Products

Located at number 1a Laburnum Avenue was a mirror centre, **P.L. Products**, which offered good designs, good quality and good value on all of its mirrors. It was opened by Mr Peter Straughan in December 1985.

W.B. Kerr

In 1958 **William B. Kerr** started off his local bus company in Wallsend. The company is located on Oak Grove and is still going strong today in 2011 with a fleet of large and small coaches.

Miss Beeson

Miss Beeson was a dress maker working from 56 Dene View around 1908. A high class dressmaker she specialised in evening dresses.

Gordon Square Garage

Before we leave the north of the High Street I would just like to mention **Gordon Square Garage** (the white building to the right of the photo). Behind what were called Turners Buildings was the **Wallsend Motor Company** garage at Gordon Square, which was used as a Fire Station during the Second World War, situated roughly opposite where the Forum car park entrance/exit is now, in the car parking bays running north to south. This company dealt mainly as a second-hand car garage. My father was employed by the owner Arnold Waugh and was paid £21 per week, working with Arnold's brother, Peter. These expert mechanics undertook repairs of any description on these cars before they were taken to **Blenheim Street Motors** in Newcastle to be sold. After working at this site for a few years **Wallsend Motor Company** moved to Sycamore Street, opposite **Scott Funeral Parlour**.

Photograph of Gordon Square courtesy of George Laws and Rod & Margaret Thomson.

We now leave the shops north of the High Street and move on to the area south of High Street.

South of the High Street

Our first stop in this section is at the far most western part of Wallsend before it becomes Walker.

A. Nicholson
At number 74 Neptune Road stood newsagents **A. Nicholson**. Not only was he a newsagents, in the 1925 Wallsend Guide booklet he described himself as a newsagent, confectioner and tobacconist. He provided all types of newspapers and stationery, the choicest confectionery and large stocks of the leading brands of tobacco and cigarettes. As his advert pronounced 'We have THE BEST'.

Paul's
Previously mentioned on page 37 **Paul's** had another branch of fish and chips shop at number 30 Neptune Road.

Ethel Christer
Around 1930 **Miss Ethel Christer** established a pharmacy at number 12 Neptune Road. Before this the shop had been held by several fishmongers and even earlier, before the First World War, by local butchers. It is thought the first trader may have been **John Boult** in the late 1890s.

G.H. Johnson
G.H. Johnson's Drug Store was said to have been located at number 12 Neptune Road around the 1970s and it was thought to have taken over **Ethel Christer's** pharmacy.

Greenwell's
Next door to **Ethel Christer's** pharmacy stood a post office. At an earlier date it would have been **Ralph Potts** grocery store and in the late 1930s a branch of **J.R. Greenwell Ltd. J.R. Greenwell, Wholesale Grocers and Provision Merchants** had several shops in Wallsend in the 1920s, this one being located at 8 Neptune Road.

John R. Robson

In 1973 the above mentioned post office may have belonged to **John R. Robson**. In the 1930s the premises then would have been closer to the corner of Benton Way and may possibly have been part of **Joseph Allen's** store.

We leave Neptune Road now and move on to Buddle Street.

London & Newcastle Tea Company

At number 91 Buddle Street stood the **London & Newcastle Tea Company**. Buddle Street was named after the mining engineer John Buddle and runs west to east along by the Riverside Line.

Simpson's Hotel

Situated at number 11 Buddle Street, on the site of what is now Segedunum Roman Fort and Museum, was **Simpson's Hotel**. It was built in 1912 by Simpson, Boyd and Hunter and named after Dr Robert Simpson of Newcastle. With 300 bedrooms it was the largest residential building in Wallsend. It was built for the purpose of offering the workers of **Swan Hunter's** and the surrounding ship builders a place to stay which was close to work to cut down travelling. It was described as being 'on a Trolley Bus Route' and 'only 3 minutes from the railway station'. It had a large restaurant, two small dining rooms, a lounge, a reading

SIMPSONS HOTEL

BUDDLE STREET - WALLSEND-ON-TYNE

Telephone : Wallsend 63796.

On Trolley Bus Route and 3 minutes from Railway Station.

This hotel is the largest residential building in Wallsend, and built on the site of the Roman Wall at the Camp of Segedunum.

The Hotel has 300 bedrooms, and equipped with large restaurant and two small dining rooms, lounge, reading room, and games room, all centrally heated.

Modern and well appointed toilets fitted with baths and showers.

Excellent Meals at Moderate Prices.   Restaurant Service from 6.0 a.m. to 9.0 p.m. daily

AMPLE SEATING ACCOMMODATION FOR NON-RESIDENTS.   WEDDING PARTIES CATERED FOR.

Proprietors :
Simpsons Hotels Co., Ltd.,
Reg. Office :
11 Buddle Street,
Wallsend-on-Tyne.

Hotels under the same Management :
SIMPSONS HOTEL, HIGH LANE ROW,
HEBBURN.   200 Rooms.
GREAT EASTERN HOTEL, 100 DUKE STREET,
GLASGOW.   420 Rooms.

room and a games room. There was also a bar in the hotel which had wing doors on the entrance. These doors earned the bar the nickname of the Ponderosa from the old western television show, *Bonanza*. It is safe to say that this hotel was not the grandest of places to stay, earning many reputations for its poor conditions. In May 1981 the Hotel advertised bed and breakfast for £2.90 and a week's full board for £22.96 although the Hotel closed at the beginning of June 1981 due to 'economic reasons'. The buildings was demolished in 1983 to make way for the **Segedunum Museum**.

John Thornton

Moving on to Sharpe Road we come to printers, **John Thornton**, who advertised in the 1951 Jubilee issue of the Guide to Wallsend. They owned the Wallsend Printing Works which was established in 1893 supplying many Tyneside Industries. This is thought to be the same John Thornton who owned works in the Central Buildings (see page 35).

We now leave Sharpe Road and head on to Carville Road. Carville Road was named after the Carr family who used to live in Wallsend around the 1770s. Robert Carr rebuilt a large house near the western end of Segedunum Roman Fort, once Cosyn's House, which he then called Carville. (This may have been Carr Villa and changed to Carville with the surrounding area becoming known as Carville.)

L. Haines

Local newsagent and tobacconist, **L. Haines** was situated at number 18 Carville Road around 1925.

Tyneside Pawnbroking Co Ltd

Advertised in the 1935 King's Silver Jubilee issue of the Wallsend Guide booklet was this pawnbroking company. **Tyneside Pawnbroking Co Ltd** offered to lend money on almost anything from jewellery, clothing and household goods.

TYNESIDE PAWNBROKING CO., LTD.

Phone: 63526.

52 CARVILLE ROAD.

MOST MONEY LENT

on Jewellery, Clothing, and Household Goods.

The Shop for Cheap Bedding, Suits, Carpets, Hearth Rugs, Jewellery, etc.

T. Rowntree

Wholesale and retail fruit and potato merchant, **T. Rowntree** was advertised in the 1925 Guide to Wallsend and was then located at number 61 Carville Road. At the time of advertising it claimed to be the 'Oldest Established Fruiterers in the Town'.

J.R. Greenwell

A few doors down from **Rowntree's** was another branch of **J.R. Greenwell's**, the Grocer and Provisions Merchant.

L.M. Chambers

In the 1972-1973 Guide book to Wallsend, builders **L.M. Chambers** were advertised as being on Carville Road. It is uncertain if this is the same or part of the same company who are located in Willington Quay, behind the Jet Garage, who sell Gas Cylinders and Bottles.

Long & Scott

Local DIY suppliers, **Long & Scott** were trading at Carville Road around 1962-1963. They catered for the professional and amateur craftsman and also advertised 'repairs, extensions and alterations to properties'.

We move on to Curzon Road now.

J. Smettem

The only company we have on Curzon Road is plumber and sanitary Engineer, **J. Smettem**. They were advertised in the 1951 Jubilee issue of the Wallsend Guide booklet. His home address was shown as 23 Harrison Road, Willington Quay and he was a Member of the Institute of Plumbers Ltd.

We now come to Border Road, which is near the west end of High Street West, running north to south.

Backley's

Backley's on Border Road was famous for its cream cakes. It had a sign for 'TUROG' on the first floor outside wall as did most of **Backley's** bakeries. They also had shops along the High Street, (see pages 9 and 14). The owner of **Backley's** used to have an Austin 16 motor car which my father used to service.

James Diball

Also on Border Road around 1925 as advertised in the Wallsend Guide booklet of that year, was builder and

A LONG REIGN IN INDUSTRY — ALFRED AND THE CAKES.

═══════BACKLEY'S═══════

The MECCA for all that is delicious in Cake Confectionery.

decorators merchants **James Diball** (pronounced Die-ball). J. Diball used to work for **Moore's Builders** which was on High Street West. His works were located on the west side of Border Road, opposite St Andrew's Church. This church was demolished around the mid 1990s.

G.W. Richardson

At number 13 on the east side was **G.W. Richardson**. He advertised in the Wallsend Jubilee booklet. A family butcher, he specialised in English and imported meats, sausages and potted meat. The shop is now **Mahogany Hairdressing Salon**.

Mobile Photo Service

Around 1965 on Border Road was the **Mobile Photo Service**. My father remembers the owner of this photographers shop was called Bob, surname unknown and was an associate of **Jimmy Dickinson**, another well-known photographer in Wallsend, (we will cover Dickinson in more detail later).

Robert Brook

Towards the end of the 1860s the shop on the corner of High Street West and Border Road was taken up by **Robert Brook**. In 1871 he advertised himself as a newsagent at number 62 High Street West which means this shop should really be placed in the first chapter, 'High Street West', but as part of the shop was on Border Road it is mentioned in this section. At some date the business was taken over by his grandson, Alexander Brook, who described himself as a newsagent and stationer, selling such items as Bibles, prize books and postcard albums. This shop was presumably **Siddle's** and became **Laavanya's** (closed in 2011).

Let's move back west a little way to The Avenue now.

M. Stubbs

In 1908 **M. Stubbs** was located at number 119 The Avenue. He was a photographer who specialised in Ivory Miniatures.

Norman Motors

In 1972-1973 **Norman Motors** were advertised as trading from 143-145 The Avenue. This motor company specialised in anything for the motor vehicle including new and remould tyres, batteries and accessories.

2H Taxis

Located at the rear of the Queens Head public house and behind Portugal Place, this taxi firm was located in an old abattoir. My father used to work for this company and can still remember the hooks hanging on the wall. **2H Taxis** was started when Tommy Henderson and Sidney Holgate, who used to work for **Denney's Garage**, left there and hired this old building. (The 2 H's coming from the initials of Tommy and Sidney's surnames.) It was accessed via a tunnel next to the Queens Head.

Paul's

At number 4 Gerald Street was another branch of **Paul's** fish and chips shop, which traded around 1925.

Lamond and Himson

Located at number 2 Atkinson Street around 1962-1963 were hairdressers **Lamond and Himson**, who also had a shop on West Street (see page 31).

We now move on to the shops that used to be south of the High Street on Station Road.

Salisbury House, built in 1883, which is on the corner of Station Road at number 2 Buddle Street, was once the surgery of Doctor Thomas Wilson. The clock which is now situated on the south side of Buddle Street outside **Swan Hunter's** was originally situated at the front of this surgery but was moved to its present location for safety reasons. It opened as the **Wallsend Heritage Centre** in 1986.

The Underground Café

At one time **The Underground Café** was a tobacconist shop. The north facing wall of this café still has an advert on the side which looks like it reads 'Prince's Royal Snuff' but the words are very faint. The Underground Cafe recently changed to **AJ's Takeaway** (date unknown)

Metro Café

This building was built in 1953 and was at first a **Post Office**. At a date unknown it was taken over by the **Metro Café** but this has now closed. It was also the **Metro Motor Company**. The word 'Post Office' can still be seen above the door and on the south wall facing Wallsend Metro Station is the date stone.

Masonic Hall

Now the **Masonic Hall** this building was originally **Lloyds Bank** and was located on the west side of Station Road at number 31. It was built in 1891 with the foundation stone being laid by Sir Matthew White Ridley. It was built by local builder William Thomas Weir.

Bella Rosa

At number 35 stood **Bella Rosa** florist who advertised in the 23rd July 1987 issue of the Wallsend Guardian to celebrate the Centenary of St Luke's Church. **Bella Rosa** took over from **J.G. Anderson.**

Wallsend Furnishings

At number 37 stood **Wallsend Furnishings.** This shop would have been located between what was **Bella Rosa** and the entrance to the **Wallsend Memorial Hall.** It sold beds, three-piece suites, wall units and bed fitments. It was run by John and Jean Fisher and opened on 26th September 1985.

Wallsend Memorial Hall

At number 39 Station Road is the **Wallsend Memorial Hall** where the **Wallsend Local History Society** hold their meetings once a month. It was built in 1925 on land donated by Sir George Hunter in remembrance of the employees of **Swan Hunter and Wigham Richardson** who lost their lives in the First World War. It cost £15,000 and was paid for by the director's and employees of **Swan Hunter's.**

La Pizzeria

Standing today at number 54 on the east side is **La Pizzeria** Pizza takeaway.

Toni and Jacks

At number 62 today stands another café, **Toni and Jacks.** These last two shops are very recent and have been put in so that readers can get an idea of their location and the location of the older shops.

Lawson's Travel

Lawson's Travel traded at first from a wooden hut around 1918 and then at 64 Station Road from after the Second World War and was taken over by Edmund Hall, now Chairman of the Wallsend Local History Society, under the name of **Hall Auto, Taxies and Coaches.** (For more information see pages 17 and 67.)

Trotters

Around 1962-1963 **Trotter** was still a well known name as being a respectable ladies' and gentlemen's hairdresser. Although the ownership had long changed, the proprietor of this shop being **J.T. Dodds,** the name still remained. This shop was not only a hairdressing shop but it also sold crystal, chinaware and fancy goods. (See also page 31.)

John J.C. Campbell

In and around 1925 at number 86 stood **John J.C. Campbell,** auctioneers. This company was established in 1906 and traded as auctioneer, valuer, house, land and estate agent. He was a successor to **H.M and R. Redhead.**

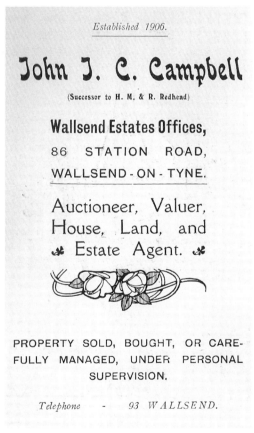

Established 1906.

John J. C. Campbell

(Successor to H. M. & R. Redhead)

Wallsend Estates Offices,

86   STATION   ROAD,

WALLSEND - ON - TYNE.

Auctioneer,   Valuer, House,   Land,   and Estate Agent.

PROPERTY SOLD, BOUGHT, OR CARE-FULLY MANAGED, UNDER PERSONAL SUPERVISION.

Telephone   -   93 WALLSEND.

Queen's Hall

The **Queen's Hall Picture House** was also located on Station Road but will be covered in more detail in a later chapter. It is now **Plaster Piece,** a fire place sales showroom.

Graftons

In the early 1960s **Graftons** clothes shop was located on the corner of Station Road and High Street West which was the site of the old **Burtons** clothes shop. It is directly under the room used by the Wallsend Local history Society. Today it is **Greenways.**

J.G. Anderson

Another shop on the site of the Memorial Hall at number 35 was **J.G. Andersons**. Established in 1893 the proprietor was R.A. Humble who advertised in the 1925 Wallsend Guide book as a high class fruiterer and florist and a member of the British Teleflower Service. The shop was run by the Anderson family from 1928 until 1985 when it was taken over by **Bella Rosa**.

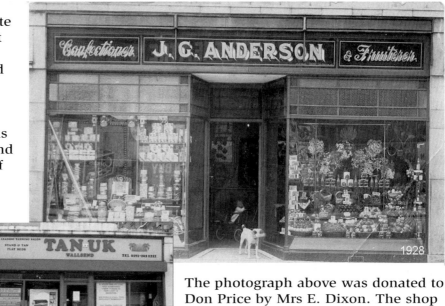

The photograph above was donated to Don Price by Mrs E. Dixon. The shop later became **Bella Rosa** and then **Tan It UK**. Photo left by Don Price.

Freddie Westphall

By Wallsend metro station, behind what was the bus canteen, was located **Freddie Westphall's Coal Yard**. Freddie had a wooden cabin in the yard and it was from this site that he set up a taxi business using Ford Popular cars. Other coal merchants were **Wilson the Coal Merchant**, who was located by the Wallsend Memorial Hall, and **Bobby Dodds and Son** who were located on the Green.

Blue Line Taxis

Blue Line Taxi Service was started in 1958 by Colin and Audrey Shanks and is now run by Ian and Paul Shanks. The taxi firm and garage were first located on the west side of Sycamore Street, but have now become larger and although the garage remains on the west side, the control room and offices are now located on the east side, having recently taken over the shop on the east corner which was once the **Army and Navy Store** amongst others. My father, Bill Boundey, worked in the garage for many years and was still working there up to his retirement.

R.S. Scott (Funerals)

At number 1 Sycamore Street stands funeral directors **R.S. Scott**. They were one of the businesses who advertised in the 1987 St Luke's Centenary celebrations.

Contessa

At number 139 Laurel Street in the early 1970s was **Contessa** hairdressers.

Hong Kong Fish and Curries

Thought to be one of the first Chinese restaurants/takeaways, **Hong Kong Fish and Curries** was located at 17 Chestnut Street. They took bookings for Chinese and English meals and also fish and chips.

We now move on to a few of the old businesses on Park Road.

Choi Kee Restaurant

Another early Chinese Restaurant, the **Choi Kee Restaurant** was advertised in the 1972-1973 Wallsend Guide as trading on Park Road but unfortunately no number was shown. As most of the shops and businesses today seem to be on Park Road south side it is presumed it was south of the High Street. There are two other businesses on the north side of Park Road today, one being the **Park Road Doctor's Surgery** and the **Park Dental Practice**.

Eric's

Hairdresser's shop **Eric's** has been located on the east side of Park Road for many years before moving to High Street East/Sycamore Street. These premises on Park Road are now **www.Laptopon.co.uk**.

Bob Young Limited

Fish merchant **Bob Young Limited** was trading at number 63 Park Road during the early 1970s. Today these premises are **Hyare's Premier** corner shop.

James MacHarg

In the early 1900s **James MacHarg** was a local builder and contractor situated on Park Road. Advertised in the St Peter's Parish magazine of around 1908 the advert did not give a number but stated that **MacHarg's** gave free estimates and proper attention to all kinds of property repairs in the building trade by competent workmen. **MacHarg** built the Central Buildings and may have been related to Edward MacHarg who managed the Billiard rooms there. He had his Park Road premises around the time the Central Buildings were built. **James MacHarg** also owned the **Tyne Picture Theatre**, the **Royal Picture Hall**, both in Wallsend, and the **Pearl Picture Palace** in Willington Quay.

Athey's Store

At number 4 Willow Grove around 1925 as advertised in the Wallsend Guide book of that year was **Athey's Store** who delivered 'groceries, provision and confectioneries of the finest quality'. Athey's even sold fish suppers in the evening and for a few hours on a Saturday lunch time, not only at this shop at in Willow Grove but also at number 270 High Street East.

T.M. Grierson

Around the early 1960s at Cedar Grove was printers **T.M. Grierson**.

Victor Products

Standing on Lime Kiln Road for many years was the **Victor Products Factory**. The factory was used to produce mining and industrial equipment. The factory had a large clock on the factory wall on the north face. It stood just behind what is now the **ATS Garage**, opposite the **New Winning Tavern** Public House. Victor Products was eventually demolished in the late 1990s, shortly after these photographs were taken.

Wallsend Forum and In Shops

During the mid to late 1960s the decision was made to demolish some of the old shops on the north side of High Street West, including the Railway Hotel and the old 'Penny Wet', the Station Hotel, and properties at the back of these buildings, by Elton Street West. This decision was made so that Wallsend could be provided with a brand new shopping centre called the Forum, another link to the connections Wallsend had with the Romans.

The Forum Shopping Centre
Built 1965
Refurbished by Land Securities
1996

You'll be impressed in Presto
PRESTO
Our heart's in the N♥rth East.

The **Forum Shopping Centre** was built in 1965 and opened in 1966 with one of the more prominent shops being **Presto** which faced east looking on to the newly built Anson public house. The author's mother, Elsie Boundey, worked as a cashier in **Presto** for a short while.

The Forum entrance on Station Road.

High Street West entrance.

The **Market Woman** statue, another link to the Roman History of Wallsend, was first unveiled in its original location within the **Forum Shopping Centre** in 1966. In 1993 she was moved to her present location, outside the shopping centre next to the Anson public house, in 1993. Photograph supplied by Don Price.

These photographs show another entrance to **Wallsend Forum** including the main shop in the Forum which was the **Co-op Store** and **Forum House**. This building was due to be taken over by **Morrison's** but today (2011) still stands as it was. The two photos below right show the entrance

ONE - STOP
SHOPPING

We provide super store lay-out, the largest store in Wallsend, equipped with escalators and lifts, also ample accommodation for Free Car Parking.

★★★★ Four star shopping provided for every department, under one roof. In fact a place where you can relax during your shopping time.

Enjoy your shopping at:-

 FORUM HOUSE
WALLSEND

Where our
LOW, LOW PRICES
can save you so much!

Around the late 1980s and early 1990s **Presto's** closed their store in the Forum and this was taken over by a brand new concept in shopping for Wallsend, the **In-Shops**. This shopping experience was part of what was then the country's leading operators of speciality shopping centres for independent retailers – **In Shops Centres**.

The opening of this shopping facility was on Thursday, March 14th 1991. It lasted over three days of 'thrilling gala fun', 14th, 15th and 16th March and brought some of the day's top stars to the area. Two of these stars were Don Estelle, star of TV's *It Ain't Half Hot Mum* and Thelma Barlow, who played the well loved character, Mavis, in *Coronation Street*. Also at the opening ceremony was the Chitty Chitty Bang Bang vehicle from the film of the same name. A competition was held for people to be able to win a ride in this vehicle.

Margaret McGregor, a Wallsend Local History Society member, who used to work at **Thermal Syndicate**, managed to get her photograph taken with Don Estelle and treasures it to this day (*right*).

The following pages show some of the first shops to be located in the In Shops – how many can you remember? Because the shops were given the same address, number 8, In Shops, they have been placed in alphabetical order in this chapter.

Aladdins Cave

The first shop in alphabetical order would have been **Aladdins Cave** which sold and fixed watches, clocks and electrical goods.

Anetson Clothing

Next was **Anetson Clothing**. It was a brand new men's wear shop which sold many items of clothing including 'Citinos from £8.99', whatever they were.

Balloon Bonanza

This shop offered a whole new gift idea for the 1990s. **Balloon Bonanza** sold balloons of all sizes and shapes including helium balloons, personalized birthday and wedding anniversary balloons and even balloons with soft toys inside them.

Bella Rosa

Bella Rosa also had a shop amongst the Memorial Hall buildings at number 33/35 Station Road. This shop was the fourth one to be opened by **Bella Rosa** in the area, the other two were in Byker and North Shields.

Brewsters Bedding

Brewsters Bedding & Household Textiles, to give it its full name, sold everything you would need to furnish your home, from curtains, blinds, towels, cushions and pillows to tablecloths. They offered 10% discount if a shopper brought in the advert on the opening three days. **Brewsters** also had a shop in North Shields Shopping Hall.

Button Box

Selling everything for the sewing enthusiast, **Button Box** sold pins, zips, threads and Velcro at very reasonable prices.

Card Mania

One of the few shops to give a unit number in their address, **Card Mania** was located at Unit 45, In Shops, 8 The Forum, Wallsend. They described themselves as 'the friendly card shop where the best cost less'.

Colemans Meats

This local butchers shop offered top quality English pork, beef and lamb. Located at Unit 26-27, In Shops they offered many deals on wide selection of meats for hoteliers and the public including free delivery. **Colemans Meats** was seemingly a trade name with the owners being Les Newman & Son, Family Butchers.

Corner Café

The **Corner Café** offered a wide selection of delicious hot and cold meals, snack, cakes and drinks.

IS YOUR BUSINESS IN THE

Dress Sense Ladies Wear

Gail and Tracy welcomed everyone to their shop, **Dress Sense Ladies Wear** at Unit 38. They were already established at **Dress Sense, Party Plan** and at Whitley Bay Indoor Market and proudly welcomed all their old and new customers to their Wallsend branch.

Hall's of Elswick

This friendly Home Bakery produced all their products fresh daily. **Hall's of Elswick** had many special offers on every day. ✍

Little Stars

This children's wear shop proudly announced they were opening in the In Shops. **Little Stars** stocked a full range of children's clothing from ages 3-13.

Livewire Megastore Limited

This was one of the earliest video game stockists in Wallsend. **Livewire Megastore Ltd** was one of the leading computer and telecommunications stores in the North East selling computers, computer games, telephones, answering machines and lots more.

Livewire Megastore Ltd also had stores in Park View, Whitley Bay and North Shields Shopping Hall. Today's computer experts may just remember the names advertised for example – Sega, Nintendo, Spectrum, Commodore and Atari to name a few and were out long before Playstation and X-Boxes came on the scene.

The Panty House

The Panty House, Unit 37, the In Shops, sold a full range of lingerie, nightwear and hosiery. This company had been established since 1986 at North Shields Shopping Hall, Bedford Street.

Sew 'n' So

Clothing alterations shop, **Sew 'n' So** had a shop in the In Shops at Chester-le-Street along with this shop in Wallsend. They undertook all kinds of alterations and repairs and had quite a catchy name and stated 'Those little Sew 'n' So's get everywhere' and are now located at 166 Station Road.

Shirley's Pet Supplies

Shirley's Pet Supplies had already been trading for thirteen years under **Shirley's Dog Salon**. This was their second shop. They supplied all you could need for any pet; from pet food, toys, accessories, medicines, cages for birds and rodents, beds for animals, fish tanks and many more items.

The Sub's Bench

Sportswear Shop, **The Sub's Bench**, seems to have been owned by John Burridge, once a goalkeeper for Newcastle United. The shop sold all of the most popular branded sportswear, such as Umbro, Adidas, Nike and Puma. They had shops in the In Shops at Chester-le-Street and on the Quayside Market in Newcastle.

Willington Quay

We now leave the Wallsend area and move on to Willington Quay, covering from the Rose Inn at the bottom of Rosehill Bank to the area now covered by the Tyne Tunnel, with the new 'Tyne Tunnel 2' opened on 25th February 2011.

Robert Hood Haggie

Around 1840 **Robert Hood Haggie**, or **Haggies Rope Works**, acquired the **Willington Rope Works** on Western Road, Willington Quay. They made ropes, cords and twines etc under the brand name "**Robin Hood**". The firm employed hundreds of workers. Many of these workers were girls and because of this they were given the fond nickname "**Haggies Angels**". The photograph, supplied by Don Price, shows **Willington Mill**, part of the **Ropeworks**.

Many people are probably aware of the tale of the ghost of **Haggies Ropeworks**, Kitty the Mill Ghost. Kitty was said to have worked in the factory and died in an accident there. This may not be true as she was thought to have haunted only the detached house beside the old mill (Procter's Mill) which was owned by Joseph Procter, whose family first reported seeing Kitty. It was said she only moved on when the Procter family moved away from Willington Quay.

The Ropeworks stretched from the bottom of Rosehill bank along the full length of Western Road and ended at the beginning of Stephenson Street, near to the Albion Inn public house.

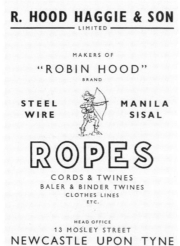

R. HOOD HAGGIE & SON
LIMITED

MAKERS OF

"ROBIN HOOD"
BRAND

STEEL   MANILA
WIRE   SISAL

ROPES

CORDS & TWINES
BALER & BINDER TWINES
CLOTHES LINES
ETC.

HEAD OFFICE
13 MOSLEY STREET
NEWCASTLE UPON TYNE

We move on to Potter Street which was located south of Bewicke Road and, along with Stephenson Street was one of the main streets in Willington Quay in the late 1800s and early 1900s. Not only were there many shops on these streets but it seems nearly every other building was a public house.

Greenwell's
This Grocery and Provision Store, **Greenwell's**, at number 15 Potter Street, was one of many shops in this chain in the Wallsend area.

T. Bainbridge & Sons
Motor and general engineers, **T. Bainbridge & Sons**, established in 1892 were located at 42 Potter Street, behind the **Albion Inn** in the mid 1920s. They were remembered for making an ambulance from a Buick motorcar. Their expert mechanics could repair any car or lorry and they offered stylish cars for hire.

Dixon's
Dixon's, a beer retailer, was also located at Potter Street from around 1895 until 1924. It was traced under Henry, Emily and William Henry Dixon. **Henry Monaghan** took the business over from the Dixons and before the Second World War it was run by **Francis Annie Hebron**.

Joseph Robson
At 45 Potter Street was a barbers shop owned by **Joseph Robson**. During the 1930s he was in the property once owned by Mary Sloss. He later moved to 41 Potter Street.

Charles Beeby Sloss
Around 1913-1914 **Charles Beeby Sloss** ran an herbalist shop at number 47a Potter Street, moving to 58 Stephenson Street by 1916. He can also be traced at 7 Coach Road and later at 78 Park Road, both Wallsend. He died around 1922 and the business was taken over by Mrs Mary Sloss who ran it into the early 1930s.

John Saunders Harvey
At 48 Potter Street between 1909 and 1934, was confectioner **John Saunders Harvey** and after that it became **R. Lawson's**.

William Goodall Barlow
Around 1901-1902 **William Goodall Barlow** owned a shop next door to the original **Turks Head** public house on Potter Street. Either late 1920s or early 1930s it became **John Thompson's** bakery.

John Arthur
John Arthur owned a boot dealer's shop around the 1890s but by the late 1890s to early 1900s it became a fried fish shop run by **James Tooke**. By the time Potter Street was demolished in the early 1930s it had been taken over by **Finlay's**. Also located on Potter Street by the Turks Head were two butcher shops, **Watson** the butcher and **Dorsche** the pork butcher. Dorsche, a German known affectionately as 'Porkie Dorsche' was thought to have later moved up to Tynemouth Road and traded from either **Carrisma** or **Hoults** the butchers shop.

Robert C. Forster

One of the oldest established businesses in the district was that of **Robert C. Forster** in Potter Street, Willington Quay. Founded by Mr R.C. Forster in a shop in Stephenson Street, this draper and clothier moved at a later date to Potter Street. Due to Mr R.C. Forster's death, the business was later taken over by **Mr E. Forster** and the trade increased becoming a very useful store with a large number of clientele, always delivering good stocks at the lowest possible prices.

J.J. Peace

Another boot and shoe merchant on Potter Street was **J.J. Peace** around the mid 1920s, at number 87. Apparently he was an agent for Comac Ladies shoes, and Grensons Men's shoes. **Peace** also had a shop at number 7 West Street in Howdon.

Fred Wall

Moving on to Carlyle Street, part of which still exists today having avoided the demolition which saw many of the streets in Willington Quay disappear, was family butchers, **Fred Wall**. Trading at number 5 Carlyle Street around the 1920s, he claimed to be a specialist in sausages.

H. Bewick

At number 12 Carlyle Street, again around the mid 1920s, was **H. Bewick** who supplied everything from high class confectioneries to delicious ices and fresh milk daily. He was associated with the Allendale Dairy. He also catered for all types of parties, large or small.

George McDermott

"You Can Get It From" was the motto used by **George McDermott**, Wholesale and retail fruiterer, potato merchant and confectioner, who was located at number 29 Bewicke Road in the mid 1920s. He could also provide wreaths and floral tributes made to order.

F.R. Kidd

Again around the mid 1920s at number 30 Bewicke Road stood **F.R. Kidd** who sold hardware, glass and china at this shop. He was a local grocer and provisions merchant who provided 'provisions of the choicest quality at the lowest possible prices' at another shop at 58 Bewicke Street.

Willington Quay and Howdon Industrial Co-operative Society

CO-OPERATIVE STORES, WILLINGTON QUAY, 1810.

This company was established in 1861 in Stephenson Street in Willington Quay. In 1891 it moved to new premises on Bewicke Road, Willington Quay. It was a flourishing business until it was badly damaged by fire in 1959 and later demolished. The photograph below shows the building being demolished after the fire damage which, rather ironically, occurred on Ash Wednesday. Described as 'an inferno', the fire started in the drapery and burnt through to the dance floor. The firemen at the scene described it as "the worst blaze in the Wallsend area since the War". The fire service were called at around thirty minutes past midnight but by this time the building was well alight with the flames coming through the roof. Five appliances were in attendance. The fire destroyed the drapery, men's wear, grocery provisions and radio and hardware departments along with the general office. Fortunately the safes and essential records were saved. After the fire an 'operation emergency' was started by the then General Manager, Mr A. Mason and headquarters were set up in a garage in an untouched part of the building to keep the business going. The butcher department survived and customers were served from a mobile shop parked nearby. The local bus services were diverted from this route until the area was made safe. In 1961 the business was transferred to the old **Lyric Cinema** on Tynemouth Road, Howdon.

Duncan Cooke & Son

Bakers, confectioners and caterers, **Duncan Cooke and Son**, had two shops in Willington Quay, one at 98 Bewicke Road and the other at number 2 George Street. He also had a shop at number 20 Burden Street, Percy Main.

Durastic

Asphalt flooring and roofing specialists, **Durastic**, were located at Stephenson Street in the early 1900s before this street was demolished.

M. Brown

Stationer, newsagent and tobacconist **M. Brown** was located at number 25 Stephenson Street in the early 1920s. He would supply all local and London newspapers daily and sold stationary requisites of all kinds, books and even undertook bookbinding.

John R. Davison

Local painter and decorator **John R. Davison** was located at number 111 George Street in the early 1920s. He dealt in all wallpapers, paints and brushes and invited anyone to call in to his premises to check his goods or any of his work. George Street was located near where the Tyne Tunnel has been built. Half of this street was demolished to make way for the Tunnel but what is of interest to my wife and myself is that we used to live in an upstairs flat at number 113 George Street with 111 directly below us. The eastern end of George Street finishes at these two house numbers today.

W.R. Brayley

At number 3-4 at the corner of Church Street in Willington Quay from 1910 to 1947 was **W.R. Brayley's** newsagents/confectioners shop. It was run by William Robinson in 1892 and then Miss Annie Robinson from 1901-1910. In a rare photo of the shop (page 56) just to the right of the door and beside the window stands a notice board with the headline "Tyne Ships Engineer Dies At Sea". It is unknown who the engineer was but the headline came from the Newcastle Journal and the photo was taken around 1916. There is also some kind of what looks like a dispensing machine (similar to an old type of chewing gum dispenser) above the notice board on the wall. **Brayley's** was described as a newsagent and confectioner shop. He was reliable in providing any type of stationery or fancy goods. The London and provincial daily papers were delivered by this newsagent shop and leading brands of confectionery and tobacco were always in stock. It seems he also had a shop at number 34 Church Street.

Jos. Wilson

Right next door to **Brayley's**, on Church Street, was **Jos. Wilson's** hairdressing shop. The shop can be seen in the photograph circa 1916, supplied by Don Price.

W.B. Morris

Standing at number 65 Nelson Street in the early 1920s was **W.B. Morris "Drug Stores"**. He supplied the best quality drugs at reasonable prices along with all types of perfumes, soaps, toiletries and fancy goods. He was also an agent for patent medicines, wines and Typhoo Tipps Tea which was a tea to calm indigestion. He also provided all photographic equipment including 48 hour printing and developing.

V.G. Stores

At the corner of Bewicke Road and Howdon Lane in the 1900s stood what was once the **V.G. Store**. The only other **V.G. Store** around this area was in Howdon and will be covered more in the next chapter. The original photograph below left was supplied by the Willington Quay Residents Society showing Howdon Gas Tanks in the background. The photograph below right is of the same shop taken in 2010.

W. B. MORRIS, "DRUG STORES,"
65 Nelson Street,
Willington Quay on Tyne

Best Quality Drugs at reasonable prices

Perfumes, Soaps, Toilet Requisites, and Fancy Goods

Agent for WINES and PATENT MEDICINES and TYPHOO TIPPS TEA (The Tea for indigestion)

All PHOTOGRAPHIC REQUISITES kept. Paper, Plates, Films, Etc.

PRINTING and DEVELOPING
48 hours' service

Rosehill and Howdon

We now move on to the area from the top of Rosehill bank to Churchill Street, the Rosehill and High farm area, Tynemouth Road in Howdon, Windsor Drive in High Howdon, on up to the very top of Churchill Street and even Battle Hill and Hadrian Park Shops.

Emily Gray
In and around 1933 there used to be a shop on the corner of Ravensworth Street and Northumberland Terrace/Tynemouth Road. It used to be a confectioners shop owned by **Emily Gray** from around 1930 to 1935.

Robert Gilchrist
At number 66 Willington Terrace, stood **Robert Gilchrist's** newsagents shop. He was possibly a coppersmith before taking the shop on in about 1905. He was still there in 1940. **Robert Gilchrist** was the sole agent for the 'News of the World' and had a large advert for the paper on the side of the shop. He also ran two market gardens nearby, probably on Archer Street by what is now the **Willington**

Quay and Howdon Boys' Club, which were later taken over by his two sons Henry and Anthony (possibly – **A.T. Gilchrist,** fruiterer, potato merchant and market gardener, Archer Street, Rosehill).

T. Falconer
Opposite this shop, at number 67 Willington Terrace stood **Thomas Falconer's** butchers shop. He delivered his food in a van which proudly bore his name on the side. He traded from here from around 1924 to 1935 when it seems he moved to Benton Way. Thomas was a member of Wallsend Council holding a seat in Willington Ward.

Mrs Ellen Wilson
Further down the road at number 79 Willington Terrace was a pale fronted shop owned by **Mrs Ellen Wilson,** a wardrobe dealer. This shop was taken over by John Mellis in about 1913. He died in 1914 and the shop was run by Mrs Elizabeth Mellis who stayed there until 1932 when she was taken over by Mrs Margaret J. Walker.

Michael McDonald
At number 85 Willington Terrace stood a shop of which the earliest known trader was **Michael McDonald,** followed in the 1920s by Mrs Elizabeth McDonald. For a short time afterwards it was taken over by Rachel Oliver and Susan Finlay. Around 1930 the shop was taken over by Michael O'Neill who leased these premises to William Redhead around 1933.

London & Newcastle Tea Company
This grocery and Provisions shop had premises at number 57 Burn Terrace along with other shops located at 51 High Street West, 142 High Street East and 91 Buddle Street.

Cassidy's

Cassidy's shop stood on Angle Terrace, Rosehill around 1929. The daughter of the owner, Mr John Cassidy, took over the market gardens from a local trader Dobson's. This may have been the same Dobson who was landlord of the **Rose Inn** at the bottom

of Rosehill Bank. The shop advertised 'Fry's Chocolate' in the window and on the wall were signs advertising 'Pills made by Parkinson's' and 'Lyons'.

The photograph shows **Cassidy's** shop with the daughter of John Cassidy standing outside and was taken around 1929. The photo was owned by Mr Michael Duddy, and comes from Don Price's collection.

Bloomfield

Baker's and confectioners, **Bloomfield's** were advertised in the 1951 Jubilee issue of the Wallsend Guide book as trading at 63 Northumberland Terrace.

J.H. James

J.H. James and Sons Limited were building contractors who were located opposite the Rosehill Tavern, Archer Street. They were advertised in the 1951 and 1962-63 Wallsend Guide books.

Rosehill Factory Direct

The two photographs below show the shops on western side of Churchill Street on the junction with Burn Terrace and Tynemouth Road. In the photo below left, taken around 1997, right on the corner is **Ashchem** chemist shop and the shop next to it looks empty. Next to that was **Rosehill Factory Direct**, with the shop next door being **Anne's** and a fruit shop on the near corner. On the far corner, the north side of Stanley Street, is the discount centre. The photo below right, taken around 2009, shows that Ashchem is still the same but **Jaff's Hairdressing** shop now occupies the empty shop. **Rosehill Factory Direct**, which in its time has been a furniture shop, launderette, second hand shop, a cafe and on two occasions a pet shop, is now closed. **Anne's**, which opened around 1980 and is now run by Roy, and the fruit shop still remain open. The **Discount Centre** has recently undergone refurbishment and is called **Premier Churchill Street Discount Centre**. Opposite **Ashchem** on Tynemouth Road stands **Dennis** chemist shop.

High Howdon Post Office

High Howdon Post Office, once **Hadrian's** bakers, was located on the corner of Churchill Street and Tynemouth Road (*below right*). It used to stand next to **Milligan's** the bakers. Both shops have now changed. The Post Office moved from this location in 2009 and is now a short distance further down Tynemouth Road (*below left*).

The old post office has recently opened in 2011 as **Daren Persson Funeral Directors**. **Milligan's** is now **Chapel Bakery** (*right*).

Carrisma

This florist shop business at number 4 Tynemouth Road is now owned and run by Ruth Raeburn and Sheila Hankin. It was opened on 1st May 2004. It was once a butchers shop and most of the hooks are still used, although today it is only flowers that are hung from them, not fresh meat. In the back room still stands the original butchers fridge. For more information and pictures see page 65.

Dorsche

Dorsche was a German butcher who was known affectionately as 'Porkie Dorsche' and was previously located in Willington Quay. He later moved up to Tynemouth Road and traded from a shop which is now either **Carrisma**, above, or **Hoults** the butchers, which stands a few doors east along Tynemouth Road.

E. Sanderson's

During the late 1970s **Mr Sanderson** ran a confectionery and tobacconist shop located at number 18 Tynemouth Road. It was a small shop and the front v-shaped entrance was shared by two shops with two separate doors, **Sanderson's** being the right hand door. It holds a special place for me as it was in this last shop that my mother used to work in around early 1979 up until the business closed.

R. Mountford's

After the Second World War **Mr Mountford** held a party in Hazelwood Terrace and had tables out in the street with food and drinks supplied. Later **Mountford's** opened a television rental shop at number 28 Tynemouth Road, selling, servicing and renting all sorts of electrical appliances from, televisions, radios, video and hoovers. In 2010 **Mountford's** on Tynemouth Road closed down and it is believed that the business moved to their other shop in South Shields.

Trustee Savings Bank

Right next door to **Mountford's** stood the Howdon branch of the **Trustee Savings Bank**. They also had a bank on High Street East. At a later date they became **Lloyds TSB**. The bank itself on Tynemouth Road closed, with all the main business still being carried out in Wallsend and an automatic cash machine (a hole-in-the-wall) was all that was left in Howdon. The premises which once were the bank offices are now home to the thriving **Vine Café**, which provide fine meals for customers old and young. Managed by Maggie Chambers, the kitchen is run by my cousin, Yvonne Evans, who always gets fantastic reviews from her many satisfied customers.

Brodie's

Brodie's was a local grocer and provisions store. Mr Herbert Brodie started off in Church Street, Willington Quay before moving to Tynemouth Road. People often went here during the war for broken biscuits which were in boxes with glass lids. You used to have to lift the lid, put your hand or trowel in and get a portion of broken biscuits out. It is thought he was the talented pianist who appeared on stage at the 15th anniversary of the **Ritz Bingo Hall** accompanying a Miss Gladys Miller, who was billed as a future singing star, while she sang such songs as "One Kiss", "One Fine Day", "Lover Come Back To Me" and "Oh! My Beloved Father".

A. Coutts

A. Coutts was a butchers shop at 86 Tynemouth Road. It was the middle shop of the group of shops at the bottom of Lisle Grove on Tynemouth Road, with a sweet shop next to it. My uncle, George Boundey used to work at **Coutts** after having worked at the **Willington Quay and Howdon Industrial Society**. Coutts advertised in the 1951 Jubilee issue of the Wallsend Guide book. They catered for large bookings, such as canteens and delivered 'rabbits when in season'.

Morton's

Howdon had a couple of well-known fish and chips shops in the 1960s, '70s and '80s as I remember. One was **Broadbent's** next to the **Northumberland Arms** public house in Rosehill and the other, my local fish and chip shop and the more interesting one in my opinion, was **Morton's** on Tynemouth Road, Howdon. Mr and Mrs Morton were very well known for always seeming to be arguing with each other. Mr Morton cooked the food and Mrs Morton served it. She used to throw a handful of chips on the counter for people to eat when she had a large queue. She never stood for any trouble in her shop and most people knew this. The shop was very narrow and long and the queue lined up down one wall, turning at the top and coming back down towards the door. The Mortons had a dog and the story of how the dog was named is as follows: when the dog first came into the shop, it ran and hid behind a heater. The heater was a portable type manufactured by the General Electric Company, having the initials GEC on the face. Mrs Morton called to the dog, 'come out from behind the GEC!' After that the dog was then called GEC. The Mortons owned an Armstrong Sidley type car.

Next to **Morton's**, after what is now a book makers, **William Hill**, was a small hairdressers (no longer there) where Eric Purvis of **Eric's** on High Street East once worked. Next to this was the local newspaper shop, but unfortunately the names cannot be remembered. As newsagents do they sold all sorts of papers, books, magazines and confectioneries and it was here that as soon as I had been given my pocket money, I used to by my Dinky or Corgi toy cars. As a typical young boy, I used to open the box and discard it in the nearest bin to play with the car. If I had only kept the box and the cars today they could be worth some money. The photograph on the previous page, taken in March 2011, shows where **Morton's** used to be and is now **Howdon Chippy**. Opposite this shop stands **Aldi** which was built on the site of the Bewicke Park public house.

V.G.

The **V.G.** shop on Cleveland Gardens in Howdon was our local shop, being as how we lived just around the corner on Holderness Road. With my parents working 6 days a week it was sometimes left to me to get the shopping in. I think I remember it was run by two brothers, one who was small with a bald head and the other, a tall man with silver hair and a black goatee type beard who reminded me of Ming The Merciless from Flash Gordon (although both were proper gentlemen). There was also a V.G. shop in Willington Quay.

Taylor's

Taylor's shop was a grocery and sweet shop on Howdon Lane, opposite the now demolished **Stephenson Memorial Middle School**. I particularly remember buying iced lollies from **Taylor's** and getting served through the small window. Some of the lolly sticks had words printed on and if you were lucky enough to have one of these you won a prize or cash (can't quite remember what) when you returned the stick to **Taylor's**. This shop is now **Scott's Deli** and sells

sandwiches and hot food with the small window no longer there.

The following photographs show some of the shops on Windsor Drive in High Howdon, the first one on the top left taken in 1997 and the other three in 2011.

Another shop, remembered as probably being the most easterly shop in Howdon, was **Alcock's** general dealer's shop at number 161 Tynemouth Road and the corner of Brunton Avenue.

The photographs above are taken in 2010 and show the shops at the top of Churchill Street. During the 1970s while I was attending **Willington High School** as it was then known, now known as **Churchill Community College**, the shop on the right was **Tate's** shop and used to sell newspapers and groceries. The small building on the photograph on the right was a dentists but it is now due for demolition. Whilst undertaking some building work at the back of these shops, there have been many glass bottles of all descriptions, shapes and colours found in the ground. It is not known where these bottles came from but they vary from sauce bottles to small Bovril bottles. One is a milk bottle which came from Joseph Robson's Farm on High Street East (see page 29). There may have been a canteen around here for the local pits or maybe Tate's shop disposed of them on his land or the location may have just been a tipping ground. These bottles have been kindly donated to the **Wallsend Local History Society** by Mrs Thompson for safe keeping. Also by **Tate's** was **Hunter's** newsagents shop.

Battle Hill Shopping Centre

Battle Hill shopping Centre was started in 1971. At that time there was only a bookmaker's, a baker and a wine and spirit store. The Emperor Hadrian pub, owned by Vaux Breweries, was opened in December 1971. The publican at the opening date was J.J. Carr. By 1974 the shopping centre had expanded and the original shops had been joined by others including a supermarket, a butcher, a grocery, a launderette and a hardware store. Walker's was the newsagents which also sold toys. Greggs had a bakery there. There was also a fish and chip shop run by I.R. Taylor. Pharmacist Mr Terence Ryan opened up a chemist shop. Mr Bob Robson had opened up a post office, which also sold wool and children's wear.

The new Battle Hill Shopping Centre, Coastway Shopping Centre, which was built and opened around 2009 now consists of the New Ocean Takeaway, Dine@Home Takeaway, Ladbrokes betting office, Tesco Express, Battle Hill Library, Coastway Dental Practice, Thompson Opticians, Greggs, Sidhu Golden Fish and Chips, Clark's Butchers, Mills (recently changed to One Stop), The Cutting Crew, Battle Hill Taxis and a bit further west, a Lidl Store.

The photographs above were taken in 2009 and show the old **Battle Hill Shopping Centre** after it was all boarded up and ready to be demolished. The photo above left shows part of the old shopping centre looking towards what used to be the entrance to the **Emperor Hadrian** public house. The photo above right shows the entrance to what used to be the **Library and Community Centre**.

The photograph right shows the new **Battle Hill Shopping Centre**, which has been re-named the **Coastway Shopping Centre**.

The photographs right and below are of Hadrian Park shops, known locally as the 'top shops'. They were built around the early 1980s to accommodate the residents of Hadrian Park and are situated just off Addington Drive beside The Bush public house.

The shops right are **Hadrian Park Chop Suey House** and **Hadrian News** newsagents shop. The newsagents shop is now run by Dorothy and Alan Cheetham.

The shops also include **Es-Tee Hair & Beauty Salon** (formerly a butchers shop), **Prince of Spice Takeaway** (once a fish and chip shop), **Lifestyle Express** (which has always been some kind of supermarket) and **Hadrian Park Dental Practice (I Like My Smile)** along with a pharmacy and **Priory Medical Group** surgery.

Other Memories and Shops

James Dickinson

James Dickinson was a local photographer who owned a shop at number 43 High Street (presumably High Street West as it seems most of the older shops were mostly listed as being on High Street, the West seems to have been added only after more shops were built on High Street East and the two streets had to be distinguishable). He once also worked for Wallsend Council taking photographs recording areas due for demolition around 1937 and had many of his photographs of the old Wallsend High Street reproduced into postcards.

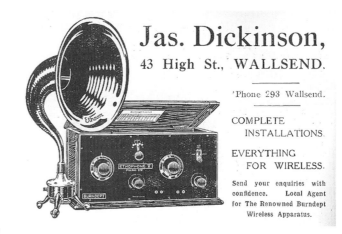

My father, Bill Boundey, used to do plenty of work on Mr Dickinson's car and because the work was of a high standard and to show his gratitude, Dickinson took the photographs of my mam and dad's wedding but did not charge a fee for doing so. The photograph on the left shows my parents, Bill and Elsie Boundey, with best man, my uncle George Boundey, and bridesmaid, Patricia Lammie, my aunt and my mam's sister. Bill Boundey remembers that the **Mobile Photo Service**, which was located on Border Road, the owner being called Robert, known as Bob (surname unknown), teamed up with James (Jimmy) Dickinson and these were well known wedding photographers.

Dickinson also supplied the wireless enthusiast with all sorts of parts for his hobby.

E. Sanderson

Sanderson's was a confectioners shop located at number 18 Tynemouth Road (see page 59). It had a v-shaped door and was the shop through the right hand door; the left hand shop being a barber shop run by a man called Joe (the name of the shop remains unknown). My mother, Elsie, worked there until it closed in 1979 and on the right is the letter she received from Mr Sanderson as a reference for any further employer, but unfortunately this was the last job she had.

Tel. Wallsend 623715

E. Sanderson
Confectioner and Tobacconist

18 Tynemouth Road
Rose Hill
Wallsend-on-Tyne

11.4.79

To Whom it may Concern.

This is to certify that Mrs E Boundey has been employed with us since April 1976 & in that time has given every satisfaction in every way.

It was only due to the fact that the business has now been closed down that she had unfortunately had to be finished.

Yours faithfully,
R Sanderson

R. Mountford

A few doors along from Sanderson's confectioner shop stood **R. Mountford's** radio, television and electrical shop. The shop is still there in 2011 but it closed in 2010. Whilst this shop sold radios, televisions and other electrical goods it also serviced them and the receipt on the right is for the supplying and fitting of a new 'boost diode valve and for resetting the ion trap'. The work was undertaken on the 23rd September 1965 at a cost of £1 12s and 8d and the bill was paid on 2nd October 1965.

Carrisma

On 1st May 2004, **Carrisma** flower shop opened at number 4 Tynemouth Road (see page 59). The present owners, Ruth and Sheila, took over the shop from Dawn and Rob and kept the name. Before that it used to be a butchers and **Carrisma** have still kept the old fridge where the meat was stored (below left) and the hooks where the meat was hung in the shop (below right) although this is not too obvious when you walk into the shop. The walls are still covered with the original tiles but have been painted over.

R. Mountford (Howdon) Ltd.
RADIO — TELEVISION — ELECTRICAL
28 TYNEMOUTH ROAD
HIGH HOWDON
WALLSEND-ON-TYNE

Telephone Wallsend 624823   S   549

23RD Sept

K.B.
FERGUSON
PHILIPS
ULTRA
FERRANTI

HOOVER
PARNALL
ENGLISH ELECTRIC
ELECTROLUX

MR Boundy
35 Windsor Drive
Howdon on Tyne

KB TV

To supplying and fitting new boost diode valve, resetting ion trap testing ok   £ 1 12 8

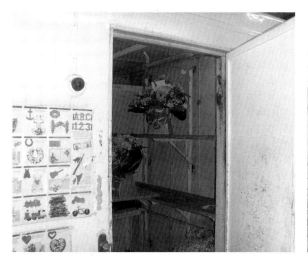

The Likely Lads

This film was made in the Wallsend area around 1975-1976. Near the beginning of the film Terry can be seen driving his sales van west along Wallsend High Street West. In the background can be seen the following shops: **Greenwood's** the tailors shop at the corner of Atkinson Street, next to this was **Timpson's** shoe shop, which was located beneath the arched window which is still there to this day and was once **Gladson's**, **Northern Rock Building Society**, **Ainsworth's** fresh fish shop, **John Day's** grocers shop and then **Macdonald's** a fabric or clothes shop. Next to this stood a very small shop, which again is still there today, which was owned by pawnbrokers **L. Rooney** and next to this stood **Tates** radio shop, all on the south side of the street. Opposite **Macdonald's** heading west to east in the Forum can be seen **Jackson the Tailors**, **Walter Willsons** and then **John Collier's** clothes shop.

Craig's Fruit Stores
The fruit shop **Craig's** was located next to Barclay's Bank and was advertised in the 1925 Guide to Wallsend.

Some of the following shops have the address as being just 'High Street'. It is thought that this would have been High Street West as this seemed to be where the earliest shops were located.

R.W. Stone
In and around 1908, **R.W. Stone** was a local jeweller who sold jewellery and watches from his shop which was located at number 45 High Street.

Book Exchange
In the 1972-1973 guide book is advertised a book shop called the **Book Exchange** with an address of 148 High Street.

Mrs George Dorr
In 1908 butcher Mrs George Dorr was located at number 154 High Street.

H.W. Flintoft
In the 1925 guide book, **H.W. Flintoft** advertised as being at Leeds House, Wallsend-on-Tyne. He was an official Scout and Guides Outfitter. Leeds House was presumably located in the premises of the old Post Office Buildings at 103 High Street West. Originally Herbert Wilson Flintoft was from Lastingham, in the Ryedale area of Yorkshire, and came to Wallsend around 1898. He traded between 1901 and 1930, becoming a local councillor from 1930 to 1933.

Roger Brand
Both a chemist and post master, **Roger Brand** had been trading in Wallsend from the late 1880s before he moved into the Post Office Buildings, High Street West in the early 1900s.

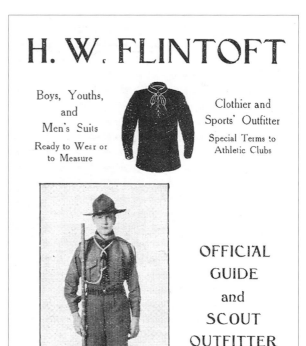

H. W. FLINTOFT

Boys, Youths, and Men's Suits

Ready to Wear or to Measure

Clothier and Sports' Outfitter

Special Terms to Athletic Clubs

OFFICIAL GUIDE and SCOUT OUTFITTER

LEEDS HOUSE 2 Doors from Post Office

WALLSEND-ON-TYNE

Other Shops Remembered

Miss Audrey Davison, 87 years old, remembers a few other shops in and around Wallsend. Here are a few not previously mentioned and the exact locations have not been given: Perry's dairy for dairy produce and eggs; Calvert butchers and Lings? butchers; Rhodes the bakers; Renwicks fruit and veg shop; Fairbairns and Corners, both shoe shops; Penny Bazaars for miscellaneous goods and Beeches Bazaar for china and glassware; Scotch wool shop for knitting wool, socks, stockings, scarves and gloves etc. Also mentioned are Thompson's sweet shop; Knott's shoe repair shop; Woods the newsagents shop; McCress's shop (it is not known what they supplied); Togneries? ice cream shop and Wilkinson the tailors shop.

Edmund Hall, chairman of the Wallsend Local History Society recalls:

The firm **Lawson's Travel** started off around 1918 by Dick Lawson in a wooden hut on Station Road, behind what was once the **Queen's Picture Hall** and is now **Plaster Piece** fireplace showroom. It was a local meeting place for the bus drivers and conductors who used to operate the local bus service, serving teas as there was no proper canteen. The firm was taken over by Dick's sister, Mary Humble, when he died. They used to sell tickets for different bus tours. It was taken over by Edmund Hall, **Hall Auto, Taxi and Coaches**, who expanded the bus routes and tours and introduced taxi cabs to the service. These taxis were later to become **Wallsend Taxis**. He opened another shop on High Street East. This business closed in the 1960s.

The following photograph was taken around 1956 and, shows from the left, Norman (Tucker) Yearm, who was one of the taxi drivers, Neville Worth and Bill Boundey, both mechanics, while they were working at **Denney's Garage**, which is now the **Forsters Garage** at the most western end of High Street West (see page 6). The sign for the garage can just be seen to the left of the petrol pump which sold Esso Extra petrol. (Photograph supplied by Bill Boundey.)

Audrey Cummings married my father's brother, George, and although living in Howdon, she worked in Wallsend for many years. Although her memories are vague she recalls:

"I started off working at **Percy Garrod's** around 1965 and around then Fred Ainsworth came to work for **Garrod's** before he set up his own shop."

She then worked for Tommy Douglas who bought both fish shops around 1967. She eventually retired from working in the shops in the mid 1990s although is still fondly remembered by many of her old customers.

She also remembers other shops in Wallsend. Although the names of the shops may evade her memory, she still remembers the shop keepers such as: a sweet shop which may have been located beside the **Ritz Cinema** and run by two ladies called Annie and Lizzie; a general dealers store run by Mr Thorman; a second hand shop by the Town Hall, which may now be **Metropolitan**, run by two sisters (names not known); Mr Wilkinson who sold ladies clothes; Mr Pinkler who was located at either 130 or 132 High Street East and who sold men's hats; and a shop which she thinks was called **Meadow** and was run by a Mr and Mrs Crisp. She can also recall a cheap shop which was known as **John's** who, after having problems competing with the other shops used the slogan 'Use me or lose me!' to advertise his shop. Unfortunately, this did not seem to work as the shop closed eventually.

Audrey still has a toy bulldog which was bought for her by her father near the end of the Second World War for 6d from **Woolworths** when it was located on the north side of High Street West, close to the **Black Bull** public house.

Provi Tickets

How many of us can remember getting the 'provi ticket', which enabled you to borrow up to any amount over 10/- and pay the loan back in equal payments spread over 20 weeks, to be able to buy some new clothes or whatever was needed at that time. I remember my parents always buying my brother and myself new clothes, especially at Easter Time, using this form of payment.

The following shops all participated in the Provident Ticket Scheme and were advertised in the 1959 issue of the Provident Shopping Guide and have not yet been mentioned.

Wool, knitwear and hosiery shop
William Wilkes, 149 High Street East – now **R & S Shelley** newsagents shop.

Ladies Hairdressers
Dorothy Nancy Beautyman, 65 Woodbine Avenue.
L.S. Dexter, 11 Hedley Street – this street no longer exists.
Nan Masters, 196 High Street East – now **JTP Property Maintenance**.
Elvidge Brothers, 86 High Street West – would have stood opposite the **Black Bull**, (number 85-87).

Bespoke Tailors/Outfitters
Mrs F. Gray, 84 Tynemouth Road – now where **LL's Sandwich Express** stands.

Boots/Shoes/Leather Goods
J.O. Waddington, 28 High Street West.
Corners Boots Store, 32 High Street East – now approximately where **Tom Owens** is located.
Lennards Limited, 45 High Street West – now either Blockbusters or Below.
Central Shoe Company, 176 High Street West – this shop is now a pair of flats at this time owned by my aunt, Sandra Lammie.

Toys/Games/Models/Handicrafts
J.S. Davison (Toys) Limited, 129-133 High Street West – now York Drive opposite **R U Hungry**.
Wallsend Model & Handicraft Shop, 201 High Street East – now **Inga's Hair Fashion**.

Wallpaper/Paint
Brighter Home Stores, 22 High Street East – now **Blue Line Taxis**, was **Army and Navy** shop.
W. Lane, 163 High Street West – now York Drive opposite Last Orders.
W. Brown, 88 Windsor Drive – now approximately **Windsor's Fruiterers and Pets**.
Smith's Home Decorating Services Limited, Atkinson Street.

Ironmongery/Hardware/Glass/China
M. Johnson, 10 Coast Road.

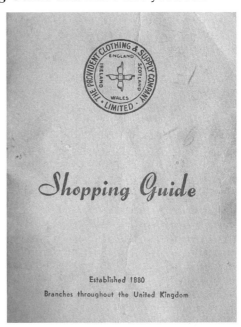

These two pictures come from an original Provident booklet presented to the Wallsend Local History Society by Tom Blaney.

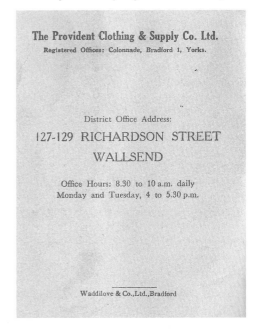

Cookers/Lighting etc
Morris & Smiles, 148 High Street West – this is now a **Removals** shop.

Watches/Clocks/Jewellery/Fancy Goods
J. Mackay, 30 High Street East – this is now **Wallsend Service Centre**.
J.M. Conway & Son, 167 High Street East – now the **Cats Protection** shop.

The **Provident Offices** were located in the first floor of the building which is now **Lloyds Trustee Savings Bank** on High Street East.

A Good Living For Workers . . .

THE PROVIDENT CLOTHING & SUPPLY
COMPANY LIMITED
(address as on back cover of this guide)

require a few
Well-Connected, Intelligent and Trustworthy

AGENTS

The appointment will lead to a most remunerative
position if the applicant is a worker

You CAN afford it NOW!
DON'T DISTURB YOUR SAVINGS

You can get
PROVIDENT CHECKS
issued in value from 10/- upwards

You repay same to The Provident Clothing & Supply
Co. Ltd. by equal weekly payments spread over 20 weeks.

The great advantage of a Provident Check over any
other weekly payment system is that your local shop-
keepers (as shown in this Shopping Guide) treat the

PROVIDENT CHECK exactly as cash

Two adverts from the Provident booklet.

Newsagents

Brooke's
Brooke's newsagents was located at the top end of High Street West, by Border Road and Hedley Street. The front shop window on the High Street was filled with toys and books and the side windows were full of everything the enthusiast would need for making cuckoo clocks, forts, dolls houses and any other wooden furniture and all the wood tools necessary for working the wood and making furniture.

Heslop's
The London Illustrated News used to feature their centre pages in this newsagents shop, which is now where the Ritz Bingo Hall is situated. Heslop's opened around 1910 and was moved from their location when the Ritz was being built in 1935.

Hardie's
Hardie's was run by Mrs Steele, who also taught local children to play the piano, selling sheet music in the newspaper shop as well as papers and magazines. (Could be mistaken for **Hardy's**.)

Hill's
Hill's was located east of the Ritz Bingo Hall on the same side and was described as being a big shop which sold all sorts of hardware such as pots, pans, fire grates and garden tools, having a v-shaped window with the goods displayed at the front of the shop, much like Arkwright's shop in the TV show 'Open all Hours'. Hill's also sold every type of stationary products you could possibly need. The shop sold every day items downstairs and the more out of the ordinary items upstairs.

Reays
Reays said to have been a newsagents whose speciality was postcard advertising and selling packets of foreign stamps.

Wallsend Festival Day

In July of each year, usually on the first Saturday of the month, Wallsend holds its own Festival Day. It is a day when Wallsend High Street gets closed off to traffic from Station Road to Park Road, allowing stalls and fairground rides to be held on the High Street. Wallsend Forum is transformed in to a type of market place with many stalls situated inside and outside the **Forum Shopping Centre**. The **Wallsend Local History Society** have their own stall which displays many old and new photographs of the town and old school photographs which seem to draw a lot of attention. There are also guided walks around the Green and there are marches by 'Roman Soldiers' from **Segedunum Roman Fort and Museum**. Vintage cars are displayed in one of the car parks on High Street East. More information on all of these entertainments can be found in the brochure advertising the event.

Wallsend Festival Day 2006

The photograph below was taken on Wallsend Festival Day in 2006, looking east towards **John Sibley Pets** shop. There are two shops behind the old bus, thought to be a 1940s or 1950s Bedford, but both names are unknown, before coming to **Adamson's** estate agents on the western corner of Park Road and High Street East. On the opposite corner can be seen the **Borough Theatre** with **Johnny's Amusements** occupying the ground floor.

St Luke's Church Centenary Celebration

St Luke's Church on Frank Street, Wallsend was officially consecrated in 1887, with the foundation stone having been laid in 1885. A church house in Hugh Street on land donated by W. Hunter of Swan Hunter's Shipyards, and a hall were also added in later years. The News Guardian published an advertising feature in the 23rd July 1987 issue with the following Wallsend businesses joining in and giving the church their best wishes: Weir, Webb & Bourn, Metropolitan, Dudley Charlton, Fletcher James – all Estate Agents, Robert Anthony – Investment Jewellers, Graham Builders Merchants, R.S. Scott – Funeral Directors, T. & G. Allan – Stationers, Joyce Elliot – Hairdressers, Newcastle Moat House, Co-operative Funeral Service and Co-operative Cleaners, Bella Rosa – Florists, Foxhunters Garage, North East Joinery & Timber, Mountford's Television dealers and of course the News Guardian.

Steve Phillips

Steve Phillips, whose shop is on Tynemouth Road, Howdon, started work for **Albert Wilkinson** when he was 18 years old. Albert took over from **Douggie Mellor** and Steve took over from Wilkinsons in 1997. Steve is one of the 'old type' of butchers, a friendly, family butcher who makes time to have a chat with his regular customers, as they often did in the past. Today a lot of meat products are bought from local superstores where the service, although still friendly, does not seem the same.

The shop on the corner on the left of the photograph of Elton Street looking east towards Station Road in 1963, is now an insurance broker, **Bestford & Company Insurance Brokers**. This company was established in 1981 but it is not known when they took over this site.

L. & M. Todd

L. & M. Todd sold beautiful hats from their shop at number 86 High Street East and was known as 'Wallsend's Popular Hat Shop'. It had a vast array of hats of all kinds on display in the windows.

CYCLE AND
RADIO DEALERS

Alsop & Sons

99, High St. West
Wallsend-on-Tyne
Phone Wallsend 63309.

147, Park View
Whitley Bay
Phone Whitley Bay 1285.

Alsop's Cycle Shop

Next to the **Ritz Bingo Hall** later to become the **Mecca Bingo Hall** on High Street West stood **Alsop's Cycle Shop**. I remember my parents bought my brother and myself brand new racing bikes from this shop one Christmas when we were young. I even remember mine being a red and blue Raleigh Olympus. The shop window was always full of brand new bicycles of all types. The shop was later taken over by **Tomms Cycles** and after that **Pizza Nice**.

WALLSEND'S POPULAR HAT SHOP
86, HIGH STREET EAST, WALLSEND.

Mr Robert Aitchison, who has lived in Howdon for many years, gave the history society the following information from his own collection. Both Robert and his son Colin, an old school friend of mine, remember **F. Longstatff**, a chemist who used to be at the bottom of Churchill Street before moving to the shop further east between Lisle Grove and Howdon Lane and hardware shop on the eastern corner of Ravensworth Terrace, between Gordon House and Stanley House, both built in 1896.

The adverts right and below are from the booklet the Wallsend Church Monthly programme, dated July 1899 presented by Robert Aitchison.

The second booklet supplied by Robert Aitchison is the 1954 St Peter's Church Blotter book and here are some of the adverts:

Jack and Nelly Hornsby
Located at the western corner of Park Road and High Street East, on the south side of the road, was a hardware and fancy goods shop which was owned by my relatives, Nelly Hornsby (née Winder) and her husband John. They were reported to have had shares in a South African diamond mine. The shop, which has a rounded front, was once **Go-As-You-Please.**

The photograph shows John and Nelly and was supplied by my aunt Dorothy Miller.

Local Cinemas

Queen's Cinema

The **Queen's Cinema** had a few names. It is thought that it started off as **McDonald's Picture House** and was supposed to have been 'the first and the best' according to an advertisement on a hoarding on the wall which was at the site of the **Woolworths** store around about 1910. The McDonald mentioned is probably William McDonald lessee of a picture house, who was known to have given a free breakfast to 200 poor children at Christmas time, 1908. On the 27th December he fed 461 more children and provided a concert and evening meal for 250 adults. In December 1912 the business passed to James McDonald who renamed the

hall the **King's Picture Hall**. During the First World War the picture hall was renamed **Queen's Picture Hall**. The **Queen's** eventually closed around 1958.

Gaumont – Borough Theatre

The **Borough Theatre** was built by Councillor James Duffy, who was once mayor of Wallsend and the only mayor to die in office. It was designed by Davidson & James of Newcastle and Willington, possibly the same people or person (Davidson) who designed the **Pearl Picture Palace** and opened in 1909.

The first bill included Harriet Vernon, Mattie Lund, Nelson Hardy, Milner & Storey, J.H. Carney, Elmo & Rego, Leslie Race and Holmes & Borthwick. It was concluded with animated pictures on the bioscope. Tickets sold at the Theatre were said to be made of brass. In 1946 the theatre became the **Gaumont Cinema** and closed in November 1960. In 1962 it became a bingo hall.

The programme on the right was from the **Borough Theatre** show on Monday 24th June 1912 and was presented to the Wallsend Local History Society by Olive Atkinson. The photograph of the interior of the Theatre shows how ornate the decorations were. It is from Don Price's collection, originally presented to him by Olive Broad.

INTERIOR OF BOROUGH THEATRE WALLSEND

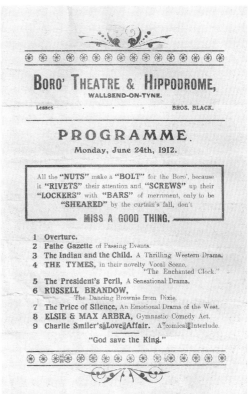

BORO' THEATRE & HIPPODROME,
WALLSEND-ON-TYNE.

Lessees   BROS. BLACK.

PROGRAMME.
Monday, June 24th, 1912.

All the "NUTS" make a "BOLT" for the Boro', because
it "RIVETS" their attention and "SCREWS" up their
"LOCKERS" with "BARS" of merriment, only to be
"SHEARED" by the curtain's fall, don't

—— MISS A GOOD THING. ——

1   Overture.
2   Pathe Gazette of Passing Events.
3   The Indian and the Child. A Thrilling Western Drama.
4   THE TYMES, in their novelty Vocal Scene,
                                    "The Enchanted Clock."
5   The President's Peril, A Sensational Drama.
6   RUSSELL BRANDOW,
                        The Dancing Brownie from Dixie.
7   The Price of Silence, An Emotional Drama of the West.
8   ELSIE & MAX ARBRA, Gymnastic Comedy Act.
9   Charlie Smiler's Love Affair. A comical Interlude.

"God save the King."

The photograph below is dated from around 1925 and shows some of staff who worked at the **Borough Theatre** around that time. It was presented to Don Price by Mrs Dorothy Ash.

Mrs Dorothy Hall, a member of the Wallsend Local History Society committee, remembers an old poem relating to the **Borough Theatre**. It is not known if this is the full poem or not but it goes like this:

'A went t' the Boro the morra,
A gorra front seat at the back,
A lady she gave me some chocolate,
A ate it ind giverit back,
A fell from the pit t' the gallery,
Ind broke a front bone in me back!'

The postcard below left was presented to Don Price by Mrs D. Thurlbeck and shows the **Borough Theatre** looking from the corner of Park Road/High Street East.

The photo below right was taken from roughly the same place. Notice that there are a few changes such as the roof line of the **Borough** and the balcony on the west side of the building. The shop on the opposite corner looks very much the same apart from some modernisation.

The photographs below were taken on 22nd February 2011 and shows the **Borough Theatre** being prepared for demolition, including **Johnny's Bingo** and **Food For Thought**, which is approximately where **Braidford's Music Shop** was located.

Below left shows the east elevation where **Hamill's Dance Studio** and the **Hairdresser** shop used to be, taken on the 12th March 2011. Below right the demolition nearly complete on 14th April 2011.

The Tyne Picture House

Tyne Picture Theatre stood just north of **Martin's Bank** on Station Road. It opened around 1909 and was owned by local builder James MacHarg. He also owned the nearby **Royal Picture House** on High Street East, by the **TSB**, and the **Pearl Cinema** in Willington Quay. The **Tyne Picture Theatre** was featured in an advertisement in the Wallsend Herald on 15th February 1909. The advert informed people that the Theatre ran films twice nightly, priced 2d, 4d and 6d, with a children's performance on Saturday afternoons. Early reviews list programmes of short films. The **Tyne** closed for a short while in 1910 for major alterations and re-opened in July of the same year, the first show including songs from Edna Gale. Live acts were quite usual and one of those acts was Wee Hilton, who was billed as Scotland's premier

> # See and Hear
>
> All the Latest Dramas, Revues and Musical Comedies at . . .
>
> THE
> # Tyne Picture Theatre,
> WALLSEND.
>
> Finest Reproduction of Talking Films in the Town.

ventriloquist, and was booked to appear in 1910. On Sundays the Theatre was taken over by the local churches and gospel lectures and sacred concerts were held there. In 1959, under **Tyne Picture Houses Ltd**, it changed to **La Continentale** showing horror and foreign films and around 1965 the company started winding up.

Ritz

The **Ritz Cinema** was opened on 15th May 1935 on High Street West. In 1950 it celebrated its 15th birthday by producing a special brochure. The Mayor of Wallsend in 1950 was Ald. Mrs A. M Hyde and she officially opened the birthday week celebrations at 2 pm on 15th May 1950. The Managing Director of the Associated British Cinemas Ltd, Mr D.J. Goodlatte sent a personal message to D.E. Stansfield, manager of the **Ritz**, which read "Best wishes for a happy week to **Ritz** patrons, staff and yourself". The entrance floor was made of Italian tiles and the Cinema had red seats and was designed in an Art Deco style. Manager David E. Stansfield also wrote thanking the patrons of the **Ritz**.

On the 19th May the Memorial Hall, Wallsend, was the venue for the **Ritz** birthday Dance which started at 8 pm and went on until 1 am. The Premier Dance Band supplied the music and 'Evening Dress was optional'. Tickets for the dance cost 5/- (five shilling). The **Ritz** birthday cake, made by local well known bakers, **Backley's**, was handed over to the Mayor at the end of the Birthday Week celebrations to be presented to the Hunter Memorial Hospital. The souvenir programme cost 6d and was individually numbered and the lucky winners received 'sundry free gifts'.

During the Second World War the Cinema was slightly damaged when it was hit in a bombing raid.

> **1935-1950 RITZ CINEMA** Wallsend
>
> **15th BIRTHDAY WEEK**
>
> Souvenir Programme ★ Price 6d
> ★ And your No.'is—524
>
> All Proceeds to Associated British Cinemas Benefit Fund

Ritz – Mecca Bingo, High Street West.
Photograph taken on 23rd April 2008 by Don Price. The Ritz was later to become **The Mecca Bingo Hall**.

Royal (or Ranch)

The **Royal**, known as the **Ranch** because of the many cowboy films it showed, was not known for being a classy place. Entry cost two jam jars and some kids were given a bag of sweets (bullets) and a toy in case they got bored. It closed in December 1957, staying empty until it was demolished in 1964. The photograph, left, was taken from Chestnut Street looking north towards the High Street to Laburnum Avenue. Also shown is the Brunswick Church. **The Trustee Savings Bank** on the right occupies what was the site of the old **Royal Picture House**. On the left can be seen the old bus terminus for what was then called the yellow bus service. The picture is from the archives of the Wallsend Local History Society.

Hugh and Dorothy Lammie

Hugh Lammie was my maternal grandfather and came to Wallsend to look for work after leaving Scotland to work in Wishaw, where it is said he made the foundation stone for the Wishaw Train Station. Dorothy High was a local girl working

as an usherette for the Royal Cinema which was around the site where the TSB now stands on High Street East. One day Hugh was waiting in the queue to get in the picture house, counting his pennies and looking a bit sorry for himself. Dorothy looked at him and, taking a liking to him, asked if he could afford to see the picture and when he told her it was going to stretch his wallet a bit, Dorothy lent him the entrance money. Hugh returned to the cinema once he had been paid his wages and gave Dorothy back her money and this led to a long and happy marriage.

Howdon Lyric

The **Howdon Lyric** stood on Tynemouth Road. It opened on 4th August 1939. It was said to have a seating capacity 1,500. The **Lyric Cinema** closed its doors for the final time in March 1960. During its time it has been part of the **Willington Quay and Howdon Co-operative Society**, before the Co-op moved to Wallsend in the mid 1960s. It has also been a shirt factory and part of the building is now home to the **High Howdon Royal British Legion Social Club** and **Nisa** shop.

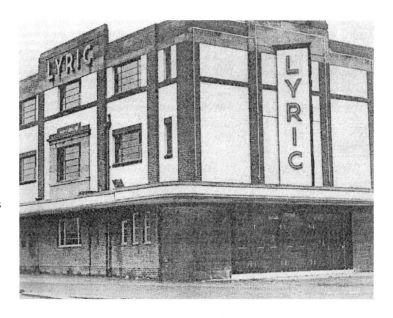

Pearl Picture Palace

The **Pearl Picture Palace** cinema was located on Potter Street in Willington Quay, and opened on 21st November 1910, running from 1910 until 1962. The manager on opening day was Edward Wilcock, late of the Borough Cinema in North Shields. Shows were held twice nightly and at the end of the night everyone stood up for the King. A renowned operatic singer of the time, Miss Adie Kaye, once sang at this cinema. It was built for a Jarrow syndicate and in October 1910 it was described as 'the first place of entertainment to be built in the town'. The contractor was David Glen of Jarrow and the architect was F. Fleming Davidson of Willington Quay.

It was one of the first cinemas to show moving pictures in the area and was the last one to close. It later became a Bingo Hall and then warehouse for General Foam Products before it came to a sad end when it burnt down around 1971.

It may have been owned by James MacHarg, who also owned the **Tyne** and **Royal** cinemas in Wallsend. Another owner was thought to have been Mary Elizabeth Taylor. Other names associated with the cinema were Alfie Taylor, pianist, George Casson senior and junior, David Casson, Isabelle Jackson and Billy Jackson. Thomas Moat was one of the managers of this cinema.

In the late 1930 the manager was David Hashman, who having sacked the cinema staff in 1938 tried to run the place with his father and an old janitor.

Entry prices at one time were 2d or two jam-jars.

Some people may remember the 'Perlibegs', a troupe of local artistes at the **Pearl**.

Next door to the Pearl doorway stood a small shop with the name Stephens above the window. Nothing is known about this shop at this moment although it looks like it is advertising 'Players Cigarettes' on a sign outside. (Photograph supplied by Malcolm Dunn.)

Wallsend Co-operative Stores

The first **Wallsend Industrial Co-operative Society** store was opened on Long Row on May Day 1862. This store proved very successful and in the mid 1890s when Wallsend Colliery bought land along North Road to build houses for its workers, the Co-op Society decided to build a branch to serve the people of this new community. The premises were built on land bought from Mr Allen on 26th February 1896. After a while the Co-op opened a grocery, a butchers and a bakers shop. In the 1970s the buildings lay vacant until they were converted at a later date into housing.

Wallsend Industrial Co-operative Society on the western side of Carville Road was erected in 1865 and opened in 1876. It provided a great service to the local people including groceries and provisions, green grocery, butcher, hardware, drapery, boots and shoes, shoe-making, tailoring, millinery and dress-making. Also included in this building were the offices and warehouses, a large function hall and slaughter house and stables. These stables were reached via a short tunnel under the archway on Frank Street, which is still there today beneath Kicks Gym.

Wallsend Industrial Co-operative Society was at one time trading on both sides of Carville Road, which was once called Long Row. The two date stones can still be seen on the building on the west side of Carville Road, including a picture denoting two shaking hands and a picture of a beehive with the dates 1862 and 1875 respectively. Now the building on the east of Carville Road houses **Ethel Austin's** charity shop and **Kentucky Fried Chicken**, fronting on to High Street East. At the back of this building was located the Wallsend Industrial Co-operative Dairy on Frank Street

DRUG DEPARTMENT.

WALLSEND INDUSTRIAL CO-OPERATIVE SOCIETY Ltd.

Bakery Dept.

Pure wholesome Bread and Confectionery made fresh daily

Miss Audrey Davison, a member of the Wallsend Local History Society, recalls:

"There were about eight departments of the Wallsend Industrial Co-operative Society:

1. Hardware and Ironmongery.
2. Drapery (ladies' coats, dresses, skirts etc and then bespoke men's tailoring).
3. Heavy Drapery (bedding, blankets, sheets, eiderdowns and curtain material etc).
4. Boots and Shoes (for men, women and children's footwear).
5. Chemist/Pharmacy (above the chemist there was a lending library).
6. Food shop (groceries, provisions, bread etc).
7. Jewellery shop (watches, clocks and jewellery).
8. Cobblers shop (boot and shoe repairs)."

The Co-operative Store on Carville Road also provided offices and warehouses, and a large functions hall. The building has recently been Dunes Amusements and Furniture Warehouse.

The following two photographs are of the Warwick Road/Carville Road Co-operative Store buildings. Below left shows part of the store with the archway leading through to the rear courtyard where the delivery vehicles were loaded up and the slaughter house and stables were kept. The photo on the right shows the same building which is now a keep fit studio called **Kicks** before and after renovation.

The photographs below show the Co-operative Store date stones on Carville Road. The photo on the left depicts the hard working staff of the Co-op by using bees and a bee-hive, with 'Established 1862' beneath and the photo on the right depicts the friendship extended by the Co-op to its customers and shows a handshake with 'Erected 1875' beneath.

The Co-operative Store had its own Dairy which was located on Frank Street, behind the main buildings on the east side of Carville Road and was using horse and carts to deliver their milk in the early 1900s. The photograph below right shows the dairy as it is now, being **A&J Graphics Garage**.

Left: Furniture Warehouse – the former Co-operative Store on Carville Road

The three adverts below all show parts of the **Co-operative Society Ltd** in Wallsend.

WALLSEND INDUSTRIAL
Co-operative Society Ltd.

Established 1862

Tel. 623341-2-3 Wallsend

Membership **21,000**

Share Capital **£900,000**

Annual Sales over **£2,000,000**

**APPROXIMATELY £200,000 PAID
EACH YEAR IN DIVIDEND TO
MEMBERS.**

JOIN NOW ! AND PARTICIPATE IN ALL THE BENEFITS.

★ DIVIDEND ON **ALL** PURCHASES.

★ **FREE** DEATH BENEFIT INSURANCE.

OLD MEMBERS, A RE-UNION IS HELD EACH EASTER.

CONVALESCENT BENEFIT AT GILSLAND.

Co-Operative Laundries,
LIMITED.

LAUNDERERS.

**CLEANERS
AND DYERS.**

Telephone or Post Card for Van to Call.

BAKERY DEPARTMENT.

WALLSEND INDUSTRIAL CO-OPERATIVE SOCIETY
Ltd.

Bakery Dept.

Wedding, Birthday and Christening Cakes are noted for Quality and Price

Also we cater for all kinds of Parties, large or small. Ask our terms before going elsewhere. You will be surprised and delighted

The Carville branch of the **Co-operative Industrial Society** (*left*) was located on the south side of Neptune Road and was built and opened in 1902. The building was built by the Co-operative Society's own building department. It was a huge building and had the 1902 date stone on the top of the building.

The Co-operative Store was also trading at the corner of North Road and Lisle Street (*left*) advertising bread and confectionery goods 'fresh daily'. The photograph below left shows the building today and it is now an empty, boarded up building. The photograph below right shows the Coach Road Branch, which was opened around 1902.

The Coach Road branch was located just opposite the Wallsend Baths, south of the Coach and Horses public house. The Society is still advertised on the outside of the building, which is now the Wallsend Engineers Social Club. On the front of the building can still be seen the sign for the Co-operative Store and Caretaker's House.

On the corner of Coach Road and Vine Street, opposite the old Wallsend Baths, can just be seen the sign for the Drug and Dispensing Department painted on the wall (*right*).

In the 1920s the form of transport used by the Co-op was often a horse and cart. One of these horse and carts was owned by Charles Lewis and used in the laundry department. He was also using his cart for milk delivery from the **Laburnum Dairies** and in 1939 his son, Norman, seemed to have continued the Laburnum Dairy deliveries in a more modern form of transport, a motor car. **Laburnum Dairies** and the **Frank Street Dairies** were not the only milk depots in Wallsend.

The Co-operative Industrial Society also had a Laundry department with its own transport which around the 1920s was horse and cart delivery.

The Co-operative Store also had a dairy on West Street (*below*) which was demolished in 2009/2010 and replaced by a sheltered housing building called Hadrian House which was opened in Spring 2011.

The Co-operative Industrial Society also had its own funeral services (*below*) which took over the premises at the west end of High Street West, in the building which was once **Hardys** (see page 10). The building which has now been painted white was built in 1924 with the date stone on the southern face of the building overlooking High Street West.

Bella Graham, my mother-in-law, kindly lent the History Society a copy of the July 1911 issue of 'The Wheatsheaf' which was a monthly record and magazine issued by the Wallsend Industrial Co-operative Society.

This page show some of the adverts featured in the July 1911 issue of 'The Wheatsheaf' magazine.

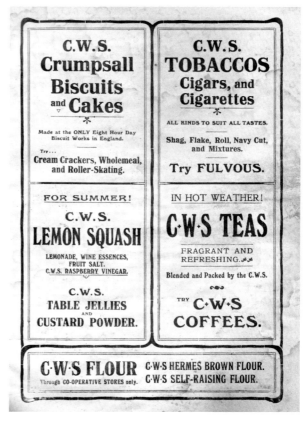

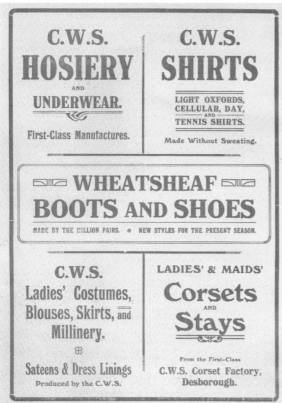

More information can be obtained about the Co-operative Society in the 'History and Handbook 1862-1912' which was published by the Wallsend Industrial Co-operative Society in 1912.

The **Willington Quay and Howdon Industrial Society** was established in 1861 in Stephenson Street in Willington Quay. In 1891 it moved to new premises on Bewicke Road, Willington Quay. It was a flourishing business until it was badly damaged by fire in 1959. In 1961 the business was transferred to the old **Lyric Cinema** on Tynemouth Road, Howdon. In 1967 this branch merged with the Wallsend branch moving away from Howdon to its new premises in the newly built Wallsend Forum. My uncle, George Boundey, used to work for the Willington Quay Co-op store in the butchers department before moving to **Coutts** butchers shop on Tynemouth Road.

Wallsend Co-operative Society was grouped under Blyth even though it was two years older. The Co-op operated stores in Willington Quay, which burnt down in 1959 and Howdon in the old Lyric Theatre. These two societies were taken over by Wallsend branch in 1967.

The photograph right which was presented to Don Price by Mrs Moira Simpson was of the **Willington Quay and Howdon Industrial Society** Butchering department showing some of the workers and their delivery vehicle. The date of the photograph is unknown but it is thought to have been around the early 1900s.

There was also a branch of the Co-op, known as the **Rosehill Co-operative Store** and was located at the junction of Stanley Street and Shakespeare Street.

Today's **Co-operative Store**, which was bought by **Morrison's** in the hope of building a much needed supermarket in Wallsend, remains empty. The Forum shopping centre, taken over by New River Retail, a Guernsey-based developer, around December 2010, is due for a complete revamp in around 2012/13 with new retailers moving in and opening up in autumn 2013. The houses in Hedley Place will have to be demolished to make way for this development. The photograph above shows how the Co-operative Store looked not too long ago but now it is without the name displayed on the side – looking south from the corner of Station Road and Hawthorn Grove. This building also held a dance floor on the upper story and it was here that I held my 18th birthday party in December 1978. The Co-operative Store along with its name may well be long gone from Wallsend but it will hopefully be remembered for a long time to come.

Conclusion

The shops and businesses mentioned in this book do not cover every single shop or business that ever traded in Wallsend. There have been many, many more, much too numerous to mention. Some have lasted over a long period of time while others have not been so fortunate and have only lasted a short while.

It is hoped that the information given in this book is true but most of it is reliant on people's memories. If there are any mistakes an apology is made here and now. There has been some references taken from local records but to have searched all of the records for all of the businesses would have been a mammoth task and not one which was intended for this project.

Many thanks go to all of the people who gave information to write this book, especially the members of the Wallsend Local History Society, Tom Blaney and Robert Aitchison.

Also I would like to thank Malcolm Dunn, George Laws, the Wallsend Guardian for information and old adverts from their archives, and Wallsend Council, now North Tyneside Council, for old adverts from their 1901-51 Jubilee Wallsend Guide and the 1925 and 1962-63 Guide to Wallsend booklets.

I would like to think I might have thanked everyone who helped with this project … if I have forgotten anyone then I make another apology now.

It may be just me but it seems that the shops of yesterday were a lot more friendly and trustworthy and on a more personal level, with many shop-owners being 'closer' to his/her customers, although many of the local 'corner shops' still maintain their friendly service to their customers. It seems there was no sign or need for CCTV cameras or security staff walking round the shops in those days in contrast to today's environment where almost every shop is now covered by some sort of alarm system or camera.

Wallsend today needs something to revitalise the High Street. There are far too many shops closing down due to the current recession. **Morrisons** coming to Wallsend as it was hoped would have been a big help to boost the area but it has been announced in May 2011 that **Morrisons** has finally confirmed that it will not be opening a new store in Wallsend and will be looking for a buyer for the old Co-op store. However there are thought to be plans to fully refurbish the Forum Shopping Centre in the near future.

In January 2011, it was announced that **Asda** would be taking over the **Netto** store, which is located on the corner of Station Road and Buddle Street, next door to the Careers Centre and this store opened on 12th October 2011. Let's hope that Wallsend can build itself back up and become the thriving town that it once was.

At the time this book was written the shops of today were correct but as time moves on some of these shops have now closed or changed hands, unfortunately an all too familiar sight nowadays which makes it difficult to keep up with recent changes.

This is meant to be a personal view of the history of Wallsend's shops and not a precise history.

Steve Boundey
Wallsend, 2011

Acknowledgements

I would like to thank the following people for their help in this project:

My wife, Audrey Boundey.

My sons, Daniel and Jack.

My father, William Boundey for his valuable help.

My brother, Billy Boundey.

A special thank you to Margaret Price, Wallsend Local History Society.

Edmund Hall, Ken Hutchinson and all the members of
the Wallsend Local History Society.

Sandra Lammie and Dorothy Miller, aunts.

George and Audrey Boundey, cousin and aunt.

Tom Blaney for his information.

Mr George Nairn, Mrs D. Thurlbeck, Mrs Dorothy Ash, Mrs E. Williams,
Mr George Laws, Olive Broad, Mrs Moira Simpson, Bella Graham,
Audrey Davison, Olive Atkinson and Rod & Margaret Thomson
for photographs and information.

Mr Robert Aitchison for his memories and information.

Thank you to Malcolm Dunn once again for his help.

Also many thanks to all others, too numerous to mention by name,
who helped provide valuable information.

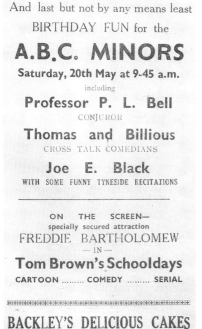

Historical Sources

The Wallsend Local History Society archives
The 1901-1951 Jubilee issue of the Guide to Wallsend
The 1925 issue of the Guide to Wallsend
The 1962-1963 issue of the Guide to Wallsend
The 1951 Jubilee Celebrations Booklet
Old copies of the News Guardian/Wallsend News
The 1946 issue of the Wallsend Town's People's Bulletin
The 1910-1935 issue of the King's Silver Jubilee Brochure
The 1959 Provident Company Shopping Guide Booklet
The Wallsend Church Monthly programme, dated July 1899
The 1954 St Peter's Church Blotter book
Ritz Cinema 15th Birthday Celebration Brochure, 1935-1950
St Peter's Parish Magazine
Don Price's 'Wallsend Bygone Days' 2010 CD

Index

The shops and businesses covered in this project are all listed below. Some of them have been known by slightly differing names such as Alsops or Alsop's Cycle Shop, both names referring to the same shop, so have been entered in the index twice and some shops names are duplicated because they have different premises.

Denney's Motors, High Street West 6
Dennis, Tynemouth Road, Howdon 58
Dine@Home Takeaway, Coastway Shopping Centre 62
Direct Supplies, 41 High Street East 21
Discount Centre, Churchill Street, Howdon 58
Disque Records, High Street East 22
Dixon's, Potter Street, Willington Quay 52
Dodds Brothers, 114 High Street East 24
Dorothy Nancy Beautyman, 65 Woodbine Avenue 68
Dorsche, Potter Street, Willington Quay 52
Dorsche, Tynemouth Road, Howdon 59
Douggie Mellor, Tynemouth Road 71
Dream Hair, 159 High Street East 26
Dress Sense Ladies Wear, Unit 38, 8 The Forum 50
Dudley Charlton, Wallsend 21
Duncan Cooke and Son, 98 Bewicke Road, Willington Quay 55
Duncan Cooke and Son, 2 George Street, Willington Quay 55
Dunes Amusements, Carville Road 80
Durastic, Stephenson Street, Willington Quay 55
E.A. Overton, 9 Grey Street 36
E. Findlay, 147 High Street West 8
E. Hay, 54 High Street West 11
E. Sanderson, 18 Tynemouth Road, Howdon 59
Edward Findlay, 56 Clyde Street 33
Elvidge Brothers, 86 High Street West 68
Emily Gray, Ravensworth Street, Rosehill 57
Emersons Pet and Garden Centre, High Street West 8
Emperor Hadrian, Battle Hill Shopping Centre, Battle Hill 62
Eric's, High Street East 18
Eric's, Park Road 46
Eric Bowran, Kings Road 36
Es-Tee Hair & Beauty Salon, Hadrian Park 63
Ethel Austin's, High Street West 80
Evening News, 12 High Street East 17
F. Longstaff, Churchill Street 72
F.R. Kidd, 30 Bewicke Road, Willington Quay 53
F.R. Kidd, 58 Bewicke Street, Willington Quay 53
F. Murphy, High Street West 13
F. Robson & Co, High Street West 12
Fairbairns, High Street East 19
Finlay's, Potter Street, Willington Quay 52
Fletcher James, Station Road 26
Food For Thought, High Street East 76
Forum House, Forum Shopping Centre 48
Forum Shopping Centre, 47
Forster's Garage, High Street West 6
Foster & Hornsby, 17 High Street East 19
Fotosnaps, 24 High Street East 20
Francis Annie Hebron, Potter Street, Willington Quay 52
Frank Street Dairies, Frank Street 83
Fred Ainsworth, 78 High Street East 24
Fred Jewitt, 76 High Street East 23
Fred Wall, 5 Carlyle Street, Willington Quay 53
Freddie Westphall's Coal Yard, Wallsend metro station 45

Frosts, Hepple Cottages 72
Furniture Link, 130 High Street East 25
Furniture Warehouse, Carville Road 80
G.H. Johnson's, 12 Neptune Road 39
G.H. Parr, 209-211 High Street East 28
G. Marchi, 125 High Street West 9
G.W. Dodds & Company, 1 North Road 32
G.W. Harrison, 95 High Street West 10
G.W. Richardson, 13 Border Road 42
Garland & Company, 146 High Street East 25
Gaumont Cinema, High Street East 74
George Gray, 39 Hedley Street 32
George Hill and Sons, 11 High Street East 19
George McDermott, 29 Bewicke Road, Willington Quay 53
George Romaine, High Street West 7
Giles, 182 High Street East 27
Gladson's, High Street West 12
Go-As-You-Please, High Street East 22
Gordon Square Garage, Gordon Square 38
Graftons, High Street West 15
Graftons, Station Road 44
Graham Builders Merchants, Wallsend 70
Greenways, Station Road 44
Greenwell's, High Street West 9
Greenwell's, 15 Potter Street, Willington Quay 52
Greenwoods, High Street West 14
Greggs, Battle Hill Shopping Centre 62
Greggs, Coastway Shopping Centre, Battle Hill 62
Gwen Jones, 82 High Street East 24
H. Bewick, 12 Carlyle Street, Willington Quay 53
H. Thomson, High Street East 30
H.W. Flintoft, Leeds House 66
Hadrian Grocers, High Street West 13
Hadrian News, Hadrian Park 63
Hadrian Park Chop Suey House, Hadrian Park 63
Hadrian Park Dental Practice, Hadrian Park 63
Hadrian Self-Service Grocery, 31 High Street West 13
Hadrian Supply Company, 31 High Street West 13
Haggies Rope Works, Western Road, Willington Quay 51
Hairdresser, High Street East 76
Hair Salon, 75 High Street East 23
Hall Auto, Taxies and Coaches, Station Road 67
Hall's of Elswick, Forum Shopping Centre 50
Hamill School of Dancing, 75 High Street East 23
Hardy, 109 High Street West 10
Hardie's, High Street West 69
Hatfields Pet Stores, 134 Station Road 33
Hedley Street Meat Mart, 14 Hedley Street 32
Henry Keedy, 78 High Street East 23
Henry Monaghan, Potter Street, Willington Quay 52
Hepworth's, High Street West 14
Heslop's , High Street West 69
High Howdon Post Office, Churchill Street, Howdon 59
Hilda Birkett, 151 High Street East 26
Hill's, High Street West 69
Hollings' Garage, 57 North Road 32

Hong Kong Fish and Curries, 17 Chestnut Street 45
Hoults, Tynemouth Road, Howdon 59
Howdon Chippy, Tynemouth Road, Howdon 61
Howdon Lyric, Tynemouth Road, Howdon 79
Hunters Newsagents Shop, Churchill Street, Howdon 62
Hyare's Premier, 63 Park Road 46
Inga's Hair Fashion, 201 High Street East 68
In-Shops, Forum Shopping Centre, High Street West 48
I.R. Taylor, Battle Hill Shopping Centre, Battle Hill 62
J. & R. Millar's, High Street East 25
J. & W.O. Brown, 143 High Street West 8
J. & W.O. Brown, 1 Birkett Street 31
J. Dampney and Co, High Street East 19
J. G. Andersons, 35 Station Road 45
J. Hickleton, 47 West Street 31
J. High, 151 High Street East 26
J.H. James and Sons Limited, Archer Street, Rosehill 58
J.H. McKean, 8 Charlotte Street 36
J.J. Duds, 78 High Street East 24
J.J. Peace, 87 Potter Street, Willington Quay 53
J.J. Peace, 7 West Street, Howdon 53
J.M. Conway & Son, 167 High Street East 69
J. Mackay, 30 High Street East 69
J. McDonald, High Street East 18
J. Moore, 183 High Street West 7
J. Newell, 14 Hedley Street 32
J. Ogston, 29 Elton Street West 32
J.O. Waddington, 28 High Street West 68
J.R. Greenwell Ltd, 8 Neptune Road 39
J.R. Greenwell's, Carville Road 41
J. Smettem, Curzon Road 41
J.S. Davison (Toys) Limited, 129-133 High Street West 68
J.T. Branley's, 34 High Street East 20
J.T. Dodds, Station Road 44
JTP Property Maintenance, 196 High Street East 68
J.W. Wilson, 204 High Street East 28
Jackdaw Café, Station Road 33
Jackson the Tailors, High Street West 65
Jaff's Hairdressing, Churchill Street, Howdon 58
James Dickinson, 43 High Street West 12
James Dickinson, 43 High Street 64
James Diball, Border Road 42
James MacHarg, Park Road 46
James Tooke, Potter Street, Willington Quay 52
James Wilson, 2a Richardson Street 37
Jeavons, 26 High Street East 20
Jennie Dunn, 9 Hedley Street 31
Jet Amusements, High Street East 19
Jewellery By Design, 138 Station Road 34
John Arthur, Potter Street, Willington Quay 52
John Collier's, High Street West 65
John Day, High Street East 26
John Day, High Street West 65
John J. C. Campbell, 86 Station Road 44
John J. Simpson, 170 High Street West 7
John Lewis Holme, 91 High Street West 11

John McCreesh, 60 High Street East 22
John Milne, High Street West 13
John Ogden's Funeral Service, High Street West 14
John Richardson's, High Street East 17
John R. Davison, 111 George Street, Willington Quay 55
John R. Robson, Neptune Road 40
John Rochester and Sons, Clyde Street 32
John's, Wallsend 67
John Saunders Harvey, 48 Potter Street, Willington Quay 52
John Sibley Pets, High Street East 22
John Sibley Pets, High Street West 70
John Thompson, Potter Street, Willington Quay 52
John Thornton Printers Ltd, Central Buildings 35
John Thornton, Sharpe Road 41
John Wilkinson, High Street West 8
Johnny's Amusements, High Street East 70
Johnny's Bingo, High Street East 76
Joseph Allen's, Neptune Road 40
Joseph Harbit, 32 High Street West 25
Joseph Mullen, Church Bank 37
Joseph Robson, High Street East 29
Joseph Robson, 45 Potter Street, Willington Quay 52
Jos. Wilson's, Church Street, Willington Quay 56
Joyce Elliot, 142 Station Road 34
Kay's, 30 High Street East 20
Kentucky Fried Chicken, High Street West 80
Kicks Gym, Frank Street, 81
King's Picture Hall, Station Road 74
Knotts Shoe Repair, Wallsend 66
L. Haines, 18 Carville Road 41
L & J's Hairdressing , Station Road 33
L.J. Winters, 182 High Street East 27
L.M. Chambers, Carville Road 41
L. & M. Todd, 86 High Street East 71
L&N Stores, High Street West 12
L. Rooney, High Street West 65
L.S. Dexter, 11 Hedley Street 68
Laburnum Dairies, Wallsend 83
La Continentale, Station Road 77
Ladbrokes, Coastway Shopping Centre 62
La Pizzeria, 54 Station Road 44
Lamond and Himson, 2 Atkinson Street 43
Lamond & Himson, 49 West Street 31
Launcelot Soulsby, 11 High Street East 19
Lawson's Travel shop, High Street East 17
Lawson's Travel, 66 Station Road 44
Lennards Limited, 45 High Street West 68
Levey's, 47 High Street East 21
Lidl, Coastway Shopping Centre 62
Lifestyle Express, Hadrian Park 63
Lings Butchers, Wallsend 66
Liptons, High Street East 19
Little Stars, Forum Shopping Centre 50
Livewire Megastore Ltd, Forum Shopping Centre 50
Lloyds Bank, 31 Station Road 43
LL's Sandwich Express, 84 Tynemouth Road 68
Local Electricity Service Centre, 80 High Street East 24

London & Newcastle Tea Co, 51 High Street West 12
London & Newcastle Tea Company, 142 High Street East 25
London& Newcastle Tea Company, 91 Buddle Street 40
London & Newcastle Tea Company, 57 Burn Terrace, Rosehill 57
Long & Scott, Carville Road 41
Lyric Cinema, Tynemouth Road, Howdon 79
M. Brown, 25 Stephenson Street, Willington Quay 55
M. Cobden, High Street West 10
M.E. Bennett, 159 High Street East 26
M. Johnson, 10 Coast Road 68
M.K. Holmes, 91 High Street West 10
M. Stubbs, 119 The Avenue 42
Mantrea, 140-142 Station Road 34
Maple Textiles, 42 High Street West 12
Marcel, 169 High Street East 26
Martins Bank, High Street West 14
Masonic Hall, 31 Station Road 43
Mayfair Jewellers, 138 Station Road 34
Maynards, 21 High Street West 13
McCress's, Wallsend 66
Macdonald's, High Street West 65
McDonald's Picture House, Station Road 74
McPherson & Kane, 133 High Street West 9
Meadow, Wallsend 67
Mecca Bingo Hall, High Street West 78
Mega Pound World, High Street East 19
Metro Café, Station Road 43
Metro Motor Company, Station Road 43
Metropolitan Estate Agents, 200 High Street East 28
Michael McDonald, 85 Willington Terrace, Rosehill 57
Middlemast's Supply Store, 31 High Street West 12
Midland Bank, High Street West 15
Mike Rogersons, High Street East 22
Milburn's Newsagents and Stationers, High Street West 12
Miller's Hill, High Street West 14
Milligan's, Churchill Street/Tynemouth Road, Howdon 59
Mills, Coastway Shopping Centre, Battle Hill 62
Miner's Club, Station Road 34
Miss A. Pittuck, 93 High Street West 10
Miss Beeson, 56 Dene View 38
Miss Ethel Christer, 12 Neptune Road 39
Mobile Photo Service, Border Road 42
Modern Tandoori Restaurant, High Street West 8
Moffett's Supply Stores, High Street East 23
Monitor Engineering, Park Road 36
Moores Builders, Border Road 42
Moore's Stores, High Street East 17
Moore's Stores, 98 High Street East 24
Morrisons, Forum 86
Morris & Smiles, 148 High Street West 69
Mortons, Tynemouth Road, Howdon 60
Motorworld, High Street East 25
Mountfords, 28 Tynemouth Road, Howdon 59
Mr E. Forster, Potter Street, Willington Quay 53

Mr J.J. Duds, 78 High Street East 24
Mrs Curry's Albion Café, 17 High Street East 19
Mrs E. Bryson, 204 High Street East 28
Mrs E. Wilson, 202 High Street East 28
Mrs Ellen Wilson, 79 Willington Terrace, Rosehill 57
Mrs F. Gray, 84 Tynemouth Road 68
Mrs George Dorr, 154 High Street 66
Nan Masters, 196 High Street East 68
National Egg Market, High Street East 19
Netto, Station Road 84
Newcastle Building Society, High Street East 19
New Ocean Takeaway, Coastway Shopping Centre 62
Next To Buy, Station Road 34
Nisa, Tynemouth Road 79
Norman Motors, 143-145 The Avenue 42
Norman Taylor Photographer, 130 High Street East 25
North Eastern Electricity Board, 80 High Street East 24
North East Joinery & Timber, Howdon Lane, Howdon 70
Northern Gas Showrooms, Station Road 33
Northern Rock Building Society, High Street West 65
Northumbrian Garage, High Street East 29
Nova Sign Company, Central Buildings 35
One Stop, Coastway Shopping Centre, Battle Hill 62
P.L. Products, 1a Laburnum Avenue 38
P.R. Garrod, 108 High Street West 25
P.R. Garrod, 130 High Street East 25
Park Road Doctor's Surgery, 46
Park Dental Practice 46
Patterson's Second-hand Shop, High Street West 8
Pauls, 2 Ferndale Avenue 37
Paul's, 4 Gerald Street 43
Paul's, 30 Neptune Road 39
Peacock's, 248 High Street East 29
Pearl Picture Palace, Potter Street, Willington Quay 79
Penny Bazaars, Wallsend 66
Percy Carr's, High Street West 14
Percy Garrod's, Wallsend 24
Perry's Dairy, Wallsend 66
Pizza Nice, High Street West 71
Plaster Piece, Station Road 44
Porters, Station Road North 34
Premier Churchill Street Discount Centre, Churchill Street, Howdon 58
Presto, Forum Shopping Centre 47
Prince of Spice, Hadrian Park 63
Priory Medical Group, Hadrian Park 63
Proctor, High Street East 27
Provident (Prudential Insurance) Company, High Street East 69
Public Benefit Boot Company Limited, 17 High Street East 19
Queen's Hall Picture House, Station Road 44
R. Brown, 25 High Street East 20
R. Calvert's, 54-56 High Street East 22
R. Craw, High Street East 27
R.E. Moore, 149 High Street East 25

R.L. Blackburn Limited, 62-64 High Street East 23

R. Peacock, 165-7-9 High Street West 7

R.S. Scott, 1 Sycamore Street 45

R & S Shelley, 149 High Street East 68

R. Stone 19 Hedley Street 32

R. Whitfields, 224 High Street East 28

R.W. Stone, 45 High Street 66

R.W. Stokoe, High Street East 22

Ranch, High Street East 78

Raymond Swan, 94 High Street East 24

Reays, High Street West 69

Rediffusion, 34a High Street East 20

Renwicks, Wallsend 66

Rhodes, Wallsend 66

Rhythm Records, 130 Station Road 33

Ritz Cinema, High Street West 77

Robert Anthony, 86 High Street West 11

Robert Brook, 62 High Street West 42

Robert C. Forster, Potter Street, Willington Quay 53

Robert Gilchrist, 66 Willington Terrace, Rosehill 57

Robert Harrison's, 57 High Street and High Street East 22

Robert Hood Haggie, Western Road, Willington Quay 51

Robert H S Craw, 204 High Street East 28

Robert L. Blackburn, 122 High Street West 14

Roger Brand, 158 High Street 66

Roger Brand, 103 High Street West 66

Rosehill Co-Operative Store, Rosehill 85

Rosehill Factory Direct, Churchill Street, Howdon 58

Royal Picture House, High Street East 78

Ruddicks, High Street West 13

Ruddick's, High Street East 26

R U Hungry, High Street West 68

S.G. Anderson, High Street East 30

S.J. Cornelius, High Street East 18

Sample, 99 High Street West 10

Sanderson and Co., 17 High Street East 19

Scotch Wool, Wallsend 66

Scott's Deli, Howdon Lane, Howdon 61

Scott Funeral Parlour, Sycamore Street 38

Segedunum Museum, Buddle Street 40

Sew 'n' So, Forum Shopping Centre, High Street West 50

Shirley's Pet Supplies, Forum Shopping Centre 50

Siddle, 130 High Street West 9

Sidhu Golden Fish and Chips, Coastway Shopping Centre 62

Simpson's Hotel, 11 Buddle Street 40

Slaters and Davison Pawnbrokers, High Street West 13

Smith's Home Decorating Services Limited, Atkinson Street 68

Smithson's Wallpaper Shop, 17 High Street East 19

Soprano's Italian Restaurant, 78-80 High Street East 24

Stephens, Potter Street, Willington Quay 79

Steve Phillips, Tynemouth Road 71

Strettles Memorials, Church Bank 37

Sunlight Laundry, Station Road 33

T. & G. Allan, 15 High Street West 14

T. Bainbridge & Sons, 42 Potter Street, Willington Quay 52

T. Close, 82-84 Station Road, 73

T. Frazer, 227-229 High Street East 29

T.F. & M. Trotter, 11 & 11a 9 Hedley Street 31

T.M. Grierson, Cedar Grove 46

T.O. Marshall's, 33-35 High Street East 20

T. Pringle, 165 High Street East 26

T.R. Boon, 186 High Street East 27

T. Rowntree, 108 Station Road 41

T. Rowntree, 61 Carville Road 41

T.T. Holmes, 89 High Street West 10

Tan-It-UK, 35 Station Road 45

Tate's, Churchill Street, Howdon 62

Tates Radio, 64-66 High Street West 11

Taylors Garage, High Street East 29

Taylor's, Howdon Lane, Howdon 61

Terence Ryan, Battle Hill Shopping Centre 62

Tesco Express, Coastway Shopping Centre 62

The Cash Drug Stores, Station Road 72

The Clyde Street Joinery, High Street West 14

The Cutting Crew, Coastway Shopping Centre 62

The Misses Hodge, Lilly Bank 72

The Modern Carpet Company, 82 High Street East 24

The Panty House, Unit 37, 8 The Forum, Wallsend 50

The Sub's Bench, Forum Shopping Centre, High Street West 50

The Underground Café, Station Road 43

Thomas A. Douglas, 130 High Street East 73

Thomas A. Douglas, 108 High Street West 73

Thomas Falconer, 67 Willington Terrace, Rosehill 57

Thomas Hedderly, 155/7/9 Station Road 34

Thompson Opticians, Coastway Shopping Centre 62

Thompson Opticians, High Street East 19

Thompsons Red Stamps Store, Wallsend 12

Thompson's Sweet Shop, Wallsend 66

Thornton Printers, Station Road 33

Timothy Whites & Taylors, 47 High Street West 12

Timpson's, High Street West 65

Toddle In, 186 High Street East 27

Tom Owens, 32 High Street East 68

Tomms Cycles, High Street West 71

Tompkins, 132 Station Road 33

Tompkins & Stubbs, 43 West Street 31

Toni and Jacks, 62 Station Road 44

Trotter, Station Road 44

Trustee Savings Bank, High Street East 21

Trustee Savings Bank, Tynemouth Road, Howdon 60

Tru-Time Taxis, 134 High Street East 25

Tudor Taxis, 57 Park Road 36

Tynecastle Carpets, 142 High Street East 25

Tyne Picture House, Station Road 77

Tyne Picture Theatre, Station Road 77

Tyneside Pawnbroking Co. Ltd, Carville Road 41

V.G. Store, Bewicke Road, Willington Quay 56

V.G., Cleveland Gardens, Howdon 61

Victor Products Factory, Lime Kiln Road 46

Victoria Wines, Station Road North 34

Vine Café, Tynemouth Road, Howdon 60

W. Brown, 88 Windsor Drive 68

W.B. Morris, 65 Nelson Street, Willington Quay 56
W. Lane, 163 High Street West 68
W.R. Brayley, 3 Church Street, Willington Quay 55
W. Turner, 203 Park Road 36
www.Laptopon.co.uk 46
W. & T. Pearce, 24 High Street East 20
Walker's, Battle Hill Shopping Centre, Battle Hill 62
Wallsend Furnishings, 37 Station Road 44
Wallsend G And Rising Sun Collieries Welfare Institute, Station Road 34
Wallsend Heritage Centre, 2 Buddle Street 43
Wallsend Industrial Co-Operative Society, Wallsend 80
Wallsend Memorial Hall, 39 Station Road 44
Wallsend Model & Handicraft Shop, 201 High Street East 68
Wallsend Motor Company Limited, High Street East 29
Wallsend Motor Company, Sycamore Street 38
Wallsend Service Centre, 30 High Street East 69
Wallsend Taxis, 203 High Street East 67
Wallsend Travel Agency, 5 High Street West 15
Walter Willsons, 61 High Street West 11
Watson, the Butcher, 22 High Street West 14

Watson, Potter Street, Willington Quay 52
Watson's Leather Co, 65 High Street West 11
Weir, Webb & Bourn, 1 High Street East 19
Well Worth It, High Street East 17
Western Dairies, 287 Station Road 35
Wilkinson the Tailors, Wallsend 66
William Atkinson, 12 High Street East 17
William B. Kerr, Oak Grove 38
William Darling, Coast Road 38
William Goodall Barlow, Potter Street, Willington Quay 52
William Hill, High Street East 19
William Hill, Tynemouth Road, Howdon 61
William Pile, 42-44 High Street East 21
William Wilkes, 149 High Street East 68
William Thompson, Wallsend 72
Willington Rope Works, Western Road, Willington Quay 51
Willington Quay and Howdon Co-operative Society, Stephenson Street 54
Willington Quay and Howdon Co-operative Society, Tynemouth Road 79
Wilson the Coal Merchant, Frank Street 45
Windsor's Fruiterers and Pets, 88 Windsor Drive 68
Woods the Newsagents, Wallsend 66
Woolworths, High Street East 17
Woolworths, 73-76 High Street West 11
Workwear Suppliers, High Street West 13

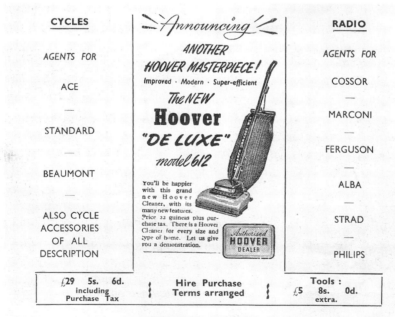

Also available from Summerhill Books

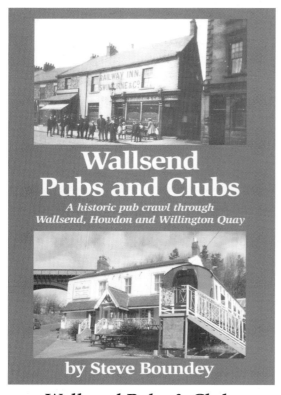

Wallsend Pubs & Clubs
A historic pub crawl through Wallsend,
Howdon & Willington Quay.

Wallsend Best
Memories of the Rising Sun Colliery
by local author, Ron Curran.

Crime and Punishment in the North East
Read about the days of Border
Reivers, press gangs, transportation
and public executions.

A History of Freemasonry in Wallsend
George A. Laws tells the story of
Freemasonry in the area from detailed
research with colour illustrations.

HAPPY HOME INVESTMENTS

Happy because they bring you leisure and pleasure. At Tates you have every Domestic Electric Appliance and Service from Radiograms to a Kettle. All well-known and reliable product-ions that maintain our high reputation and give you years of satisfaction. We will gladly demonstrate any item for you, and our Hire Purchase arrangements are designed to help you.

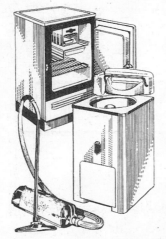

CABINET, CONSOLE AND TABLE RADIOS.
PORTABLE RADIOS
RADIOGRAMS
RECORD PLAYERS
CARPET SWEEPERS
ELECTRIC WASHERS
REFRIGERATORS
ELECTRIC COOKERS
BREAKFAST COOKERS
ELECTRIC FIRES
ELECTRIC PAINT SPRAYS
KETTLES - IRONS - TOASTERS
ETC. ETC. ETC.

HOOVER
VACUUM CLEANER

THE 'A.D.A.'
ALL-ELECTRIC WASHER WITH ELECTRIC WRINGER

'PRESTCOLD'
REFRIGERATORS
THE IDEAL FAMILY HEALTH PRESERVER

OUR RADIO REPAIR AND SERVICE DEPARTMENT gives you first class work quickly at moderate charges. We collect your Set, overhaul it, and return it to you.

64-66 HIGH STREET, WALLSEND

BRANCHES AT :

95 GRAINGER ST., TEL. 22810   AND   50A NEW BRIDGE ST., TEL. 24073, NEWCASTLE,   2 RAILWAY ST., NORTH SHIELDS, TEL 1074
6 STATION ROAD, ASHINGTON, TEL. 3264, 2 HOLMSIDE, SUNDERLAND, 28 SILVER STREET, DURHAM,
67 NEWGATE STREET, BISHOP AUCKLAND.

Summerhill Books

Summerhill Books publishes local history books on Northumberland, Durham and Tyneside. To receive a catalogue of our titles send a stamped addressed envelope to:

Summerhill Books, PO Box 1210, Newcastle-upon-Tyne NE99 4AH

or email: summerhillbooks@yahoo.co.uk

or visit our website to view our full range of books: **www.summerhillbooks.co.uk**

Postage and packaging is FREE on all UK orders.